Ski
Minnesota

Ski Minnesota

Book One:
A Cross-Country Skier's Guide
to Ninety Trails Within
Sixty Miles of the Twin Cities

Fourth Edition

by
Anders Noren

Nodin Press
Minneapolis, Minnesota
1995

Dedicated to my parents.
Not only did their support and guidance
keep me on track during the writing of this
book, but, after all, they were the ones
who taught me to ski so long ago.

Thank you.

Anders

Acknowledgments

I wish to extend my undying thanks to everyone who helped make this book happen. Especially:

Minnesota Department of Natural Resources

Minnesota Office of Tourism, for its booklet *Cross-Country Skiing*

Wisconsin Department of Natural Resources

Wisconsin Department of Development, Division of Tourism, for its booklet *Wisconsin Winter Recreation Guide*

Dennis Anderson, for producing beautiful small maps

Jonathon Sisson, for editing expertise

Everyone who granted permission to use their maps in this book:
>Minnesota Office of Tourism
>Minnesota Department of Natural Resources
>Wisconsin Department of Natural Resources
>Hennepin Parks
>Ramsey County Parks and Recreation
>Dakota County Parks
>Carver County Parks
>Washington County
>Minnesota Zoo
>City of Cannon Falls/Cannon Valley Trail
>Village of Grantsburg
>Sherburne National Wildlife Refuge
>Minnesota Landscape Arboretum
>City of Red Wing

Dad, who gave me the idea in the first place and worked many hours on the project afterward

Mom, whose research and hard work on the Third Edition made writing this book ever so much easier; and for telling me to go outside and run around after each long day of writing

Anna, for all the cookies

Peter, for constantly annoying me about his jacket

Contents

$4.95

SKI MINNESOTA

A CROSS-COUNTRY SKIER'S GUIDE TO MINNESOTA AND WESTERN WISCONSIN

OLSEN and NOREN

Preface
or
My Life as a Nordic Skier

Yes, as you probably guessed, the accompanying image is the cover of a previous edition of this book. It is actually the Second Edition, printed in 1977, whose cover appears here. Standing in the middle is my father, Gary Noren, who was in some capacity a major part of all four editions of this book; on the right I stand at age three, all decked out and ready to go with my wood skis, cable bindings, and bamboo poles (that's also me crouching on the left). Today, having just finished my nineteenth ski season, I stop and think about all that has changed in the world of cross-country skiing in Minnesota, and all that remains much as it was when those photographs were taken.

Of course, many things have changed. For starters, my equipment package is now largely made of fiberglass and other synthetic materials, and is quite a bit lighter and faster than the equipment used during my childhood. Clothing worn by skiers has changed as well, but has had less of an effect on the sport itself. Complementing changes in the material things has been the sheer increase in the number of groomed ski trails in Minnesota. Looking back through the previous editions of *Ski Minnesota*, I find that, when the first edition was published in 1973, only 24 trails could be found in the same part of Minnesota covered by this edition. In doing research for this book I was continually amazed both at the number of trails in the area, but also at the locations of these trails. Many are quite literally within the shadows of the skyscrapers of the Twin Cities. It has become a normal practice in the area to toss one's skis in the car and head for the trails after a long day at work. Thanks to a number of lighted trails, people can even ski long after the sun has set and the night of winter has enveloped the land. And the trail experiences are as varied as the skiers themselves: from Phalen's gentle, open trails, to the thrill of the densely wooded hills at Murphy-Hanrehan, to skiing among the camels and tigers of the Minnesota Zoo, skiers are never more than a few minutes' drive from a completely different skiing experience.

Thus, cross-country skiing has experienced many changes during the past twenty years. Then again, some aspects of cross-country skiing are essentially timeless; they have remain unchanged throughout my life and, I'm certain, throughout most of skiing's 4,000-year history. There is an almost indescribable sense of peace and happiness that comes when gliding along a trail in freshly-fallen snow. There's something about it that cannot be conveyed in any conversation with someone who has never skied before; it truly must be experienced to be felt and understood. This feeling holds in all of Nordic skiing. It doesn't matter whether people invest hundreds of dollars in state-of-the-art racing skis or still use the same equipment they used twenty years ago, whether they prefer breaking trail through two feet of powder while carrying a frame pack or skating on the perfectly groomed corduroy of training courses, whether they wear wool knickers or full spandex body suits, whether they prefer the isolation and solitude of a remote forest or the bedlam of the Mora Vasaloppet or the American Birkebeiner. Regardless of the preferences of the skier, the attraction to the sport remains the same.

The outlook of skiers has remained basically unchanged as well. This characteristic mentality that pervades nearly all participants shows that the insights given in the original *Ski Minnesota* remain valid today:

With the sport comes a basic responsibility that rests ultimately in the hands of the individual skier. He or she cannot expect land, either public or private, to be open to cross-country skiing if that land is not respected, if "No Trespassing" signs are ignored, and if littering is not made a personal concern. Land abuse leads to land loss. And land abuse contradicts a belief basic to cross-country skiing: a belief in the importance of having a minimum impact on the environment, a belief inherent in gliding quietly through the winter world by using only the unmechanized strength of your own body.

While this is primarily a guide to developed trails, skiers' needs are as varied as the skiers themselves, and that, while some prefer skiing on groomed trails, others prefer the untracked wilderness. Large land areas for the non-trail oriented should not be forgotten as public and private land use is determined.

United by a common delight and joy in the sport, all cross-country skiers can work together to brighten the future of skiing—whether it be by active involvement in trail construction and land use determination or by simply passing on the serenity and peace that come from a wonderful day of skiing.

And, perhaps most amusing, it still holds that none of us escapes the standard question asked of all cross-country skiers by the unknowing masses: "Oh, you cross-country ski? Isn't that a lot of work?"

The Great Minnesota Ski Pass

To ski at nearly every trail described in this book, skiers must purchase a ski pass. The pass provides access to most of the 2,600 miles of public cross-country ski trails in Minnesota. It is required by law for skiers age 16–64 and must be carried while skiing. Costs are minimal, and have remained unchanged for ten years: a yearly pass sells for $5 for individuals and $7.50 for a husband/wife combination pass. Three-year passes are also available at $14 for individuals and $21 for a husband/wife pass.

Revenues from the sale of the pass supply only about one-third of what is needed for trail development, maintenance, and grooming. Nevertheless, such revenues are a vital source of money that can only be spent on the cross-country ski program.

The Great Minnesota Ski Pass can be obtained at approximately 320 locations statewide, including all state parks, some regional parks, all county auditor's offices, many ski retailers and sporting goods stores, and the Department of Natural Resources License Bureau at 500 Lafayette Road in Saint Paul. They can also be ordered by phone, and can be charged to VISA, MasterCard, or Discover. Call (612) 296-6157 in the metro area or toll-free (800) 766-6000.

How to use this book

The format of this edition of *Ski Minnesota* is the result of combining the best aspects of previous editions of the book, plus several new elements that will help to make this edition the most functional, easy-to-use guide yet. It is based primarily on a geographic organization, but textual descriptions of the trails and parks are also listed alphabetically for convenient searching. You will find that you are able to search by region, by name of a particular park or trail, or by simply browsing through the text.

To search by region, turn to the fold-out region map inside of the front or back cover. Each number in a red circle represents a trail or park; longer red lines indicate extended multi-use trails that serve as pathways for bicycles and other forms of travel in warmer seasons. Pick a region to ski, note one or two numbers from that area, determine the page number for those entries using table of contents or index, then read the descriptions of the ski areas.

Because the trail and park entries are presented alphabetically by name, you can also search for a particular ski area by its title. Use the table of contents to find its number, then locate its place on the map. Don't forget to check the map for other trails in the vicinity of or on the way to your chosen ski area.

Some other notes on this book:

This book is not intended to relate my personal experiences on each of the trails. As I have not skied at all of the locations described in the guide, I chose to provide mostly factual information such as directions to the park, interesting features at each location, and facilities available to skiers. With this information, skiers should be able to explore new trails and parks, rather than skiing the same trails during every outing. In researching and writing this book my interest has been sparked: I hope, that during the upcoming winters, I will be able to ski the trails which I have not yet visited.

The total length of trails at a park are generally the same as the larger of the trackset/skating. At some parks, skating trails are separate from tracked trails, which increases the overall length of trails, but such increases are generally small.

In the "Location" section of each trail entry, distances given between roads are approximate. They are intended for general reference. When accompanied by a Minnesota road map, travel to and from any of the parks will be much easier. Also, unless otherwise noted, trailheads are found at the end of the last road mentioned in the directions.

Finally, remember that not all ski trail maps are created equal. The original maps which accompany the trail/park entries were selected based on their quality and availability for reproduction. The inclusion of many photocopied, hand-drawn maps (or those of similar quality) in the book would have been difficult. Most would appear too blurry or faded to be of any use to the skier. In these cases, a map has been drawn for each trail or park, showing roads and natural features (such as rivers and lakes) surrounding and leading to the trailhead. A shaded black area shows the relative location of the ski trail network. These general maps provide a basic graphic reference for determining the location of the trails and to assist in driving to the trailhead. For more detailed trail maps in these cases, contact the individual parks.

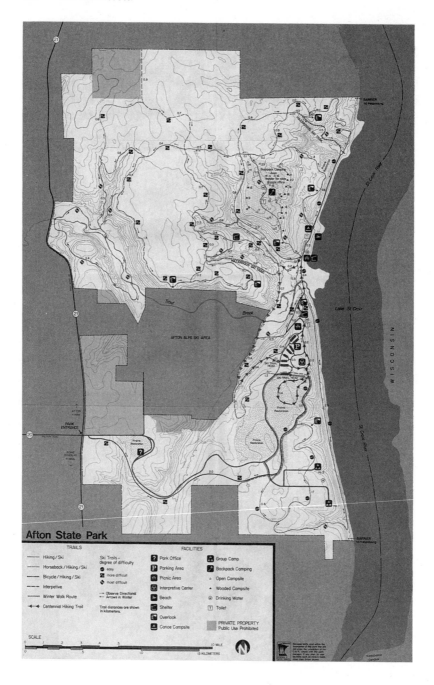

1 Afton State Park
Afton, Minnesota

Trackset: 29 km **Skating: 0 km** **Ungroomed: 0 km**

Beginner, Intermediate, Advanced

Location
From St. Paul, east on I-94 for 9 miles, south on County Road 15 (Manning Avenue) for 4 miles, south on Minnesota Highway 95 for 3 miles, east on County Road 20 (70th Street South) for 3 miles to the park entrance.

The park was established in 1969 to preserve the unique natural characteristics of this area and to provide opportunities for nature-oriented recreation. The setting is quiet and primitive. Campgrounds, the beach, and the park's interior are accessible only by trail. Afton lies on bluffs overlooking the St. Croix River, and the landscape is cut by deep ravines that fall 300 feet to the waters below. This terrain affords spectacular views of the river valley. Sandstone outcrops are common on the sides of the ravines. Oak, aspen, birch, and cherry trees grow in the ravines and in the river valley. This forestation and the rolling fields above the valley support a wide range of wildlife, including hawks, eagles, fox, deer, and badgers. Efforts have been made to restore the prairie and savanna that once existed in this area.

The steep terrain offers rugged, demanding, and invigorating skiing with many scenic overlooks on the trails. Aside from some beginner loops near the interpretive center, most of the trail system to the north of the center is for intermediate and advanced skiers. Toilets, water, and shelters are located at various points on the trails. The northern section of trails has a backpack camping area, and there is a group camp area on the beginner trails. Campers must register at the park office for a site. There is a Group Camp Area on the beginner trails. Snowmobiling is not permitted in the park.

The interpretive center, open year-round, provides interpretive displays, restrooms, maps, running water, and a pay phone. It is heated with a woodstove in the winter.

Minnesota State Parks General Information
- The parks are open year-round, but the hours vary.
- The use of weapons, traps, or nets is strictly prohibited.
- Pets must be kept on a leash no longer than six feet, and they are not allowed in the buildings or on the groomed ski trails.
- Motorized vehicles are permitted only on the park roads, not on the trails.
- Do not pick or dig up plants, disturb or feed animals, or scavenge dead wood.

• Daily or annual permits, required for all vehicles entering a state park, may be purchased at the park headquarters or the information center in St. Paul.

Contact
Afton State Park, 6959 Peller Avenue South, Hastings, MN 55033
(612) 436-5391
Department of Natural Resources, Division of Parks and Recreation,
500 Lafayette Road, St. Paul, MN 55155-4040
Metro: 296-6157
Non-metro: (800) 766-6000
TDD metro: 296-5484
TDD non-metro: (800) 657-3929

2   Alimagnet Park
Burnsville, Minnesota

Trackset: 4 km   **Skating: 0 km**   **Ungroomed: 0 km**

Intermediate

Location
From the junction of I-35E and I-35W, east on County Road 42 for 1 mile, north on County Road 11 for .5 mile to the park entrance, on the east side of the road.

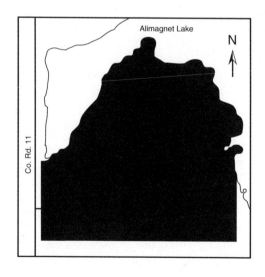

The trails are two interconnected loops: Deer Run (2.6 km) and Muskrat Way (2.15 km). They run along Alimagnet Lake through wooded and open areas and among several ponds. Both are intermediate-level trails.

Contact

Burnsville Parks and Recreation, 100 Civic Center Parkway, Burnsville, MN 55337
(612) 895-4500

3 Arcola Ski Trail
Arcola, Minnesota

Trackset: 0 km **Skating: 0 km** **Ungroomed: 5.2 km**

Beginner, Intermediate, Advanced

Location

From Stillwater, northeast on Minnesota Highway 95 for 2 miles, northeast on Arcola Trail Road for 3 miles to Rivard Road. A parking lot will soon be built on the north side of the Rivard Road. Until then, park along Arcola Trail Road.

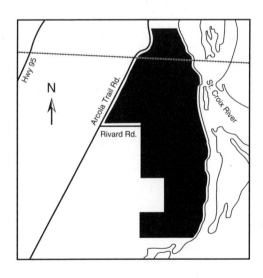

The trails run along the St. Croix River, varying in difficulty from the easy loops of the southern end to the more advanced runs of the northern section. The landscape is composed of beautiful sandstone bluffs and outcrops.

Contact
St. Croix National Scenic Riverway, P.O. Box 708, St. Croix Falls, WI 54024
(715) 483-3284

4 | Baker Park Reserve
Maple Plain, Minnesota

Trackset: 12 km   **Skating: 10.2 km**   **Ungroomed: 0 km**

Beginner, Intermediate, Advanced

Location
From Minneapolis, west on U.S. Highway 12 for 18 miles, north on County Road 19 for 2 miles, east on County Road 24 for 1.5 miles, north on County Road 201 (Parkview Drive) for .5 mile to the park entrance, on the west side of the road.

Baker Park Reserve was the initial acreage developed by Hennepin County to begin the Park Reserve District. In 1956 the Baker Family Foundation donated the core acreage, farmland that supported crops, woodlots, marshes, and lakes. Four lakes lie within the reserve, and the trail system includes Half Moon and Spurzem lakes.

The trails bypass frozen wetlands and move through much wooded land, climbing and descending gentle hills. The occasional steep hills, designed only for experienced skiers, are well marked and may be bypassed on a separate trail. There are many scenic overlooks on the trails, and the chances of seeing wildlife are high, particularly in the early morning or late afternoon.

Toilets and rest stops are scattered along the trails. Ski lessons and equipment rental (classic or skating) are available. The Baker Chalet has restrooms, phones, trail maps, snacks, beverages, and a room available for reservation for group events. The chalet is open from 10:00 a.m. to 5:00 p.m. on weekdays and 9:00 a.m. to 5:00 p.m. on weekends, when the trails are open.

Hennepin County Parks General Information
Trails are open from 8:00 a.m. to sunset. Some parks designate certain nights for moonlight or lantern skiing. All trails and accesses are open on holidays; however, trailheads, visitor centers, and other facilities close early or do not open on Thanksgiving Day, Christmas Eve, and Christmas Day.

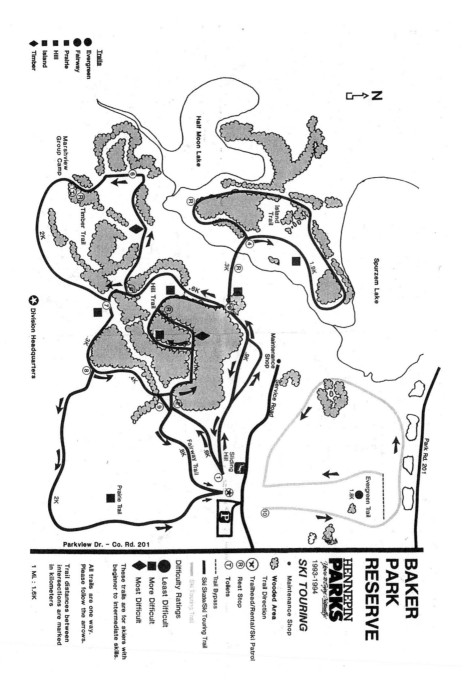

Trails

● Evergreen
● Fairway
■ Prairie
■ Hill
■ Island
◆ Timber

↳→**N**

Half Moon Lake

Marshview
Group Camp

ℝ Timber Trail

2K

Island
Trail

Spurzem Lake

ℝ

.3K

④ 1.8K

ℝ

.8K

Hill Trail

ℝ

⑦

.3K

Maintenance
Shop

Service Road

.8K

⑤

.8K

⑧

.3K

.4K

⑨

Evergreen Trail
1.8K

Park Rd. 201

Fairway Trail

.8K

.8K

Sliding
Hill

.8K

⑩

Prairie Trail

2K

✪ Division Headquarters

①

🅿

Parkview Dr. – Co. Rd. 201

**BAKER
PARK
RESERVE**

**HENNEPIN
PARKS**

1993-1994

SKI TOURING

● Maintenance Shop

Wooded Area

✈ Trailhead/Rental/Ski Patrol

Ⓡ Rest Stop

Ⓣ Toilets

▬ Trail Bypass

— Ski Skate/Ski Touring Trail

Ski Touring Trail

Difficulty Ratings

● Least Difficult

■ More Difficult

◆ Most Difficult

These trails are for skiers with
beginner to intermediate skills.

All trails are one way.
Please follow the arrows.

Trail distances between
intersections are marked
in kilometers.

1 Mi. : 1.6K

Many of the parks offer a full progression of ski lessons for children and adults, including instruction in classic and skating. To rent skis, boots, and poles, a picture ID is required. In addition to on-the-trail lessons, several indoor programs teach a variety of skiing basics, including an introduction to cross-country skiing, ski skating, telemark skiing, and ski waxing. There are also many non-skiing programs, such as snowshoeing and deer watching, for children and adults.

A parking fee is charged at all parks: daily, $4; annual, $20; senior citizens annual, $13. The first Tuesday of each month is a free day in all parks: no parking fees are charged. When a holiday falls on the first Tuesday of a month, the second Tuesday is a free day. Hennepin Parks permits are honored at Washington, Anoka, and Carver county parks. Washington and Anoka county parks permits are valid at Hennepin Parks facilities. When displayed with a $4 "Star" permit, Carver County permits are valid at Hennepin Parks.

The parks have a few simple rules:
• Ski during park operating hours only.
• Ski only on groomed trails and follow all directional signs.
• Dogs are not permitted on the ski trails.
• Ski trails are designed and maintained for skiing only. Hiking, sledding, snowshoeing, and snowmobiling can ruin a good ski track.

Contact

Hennepin Parks, 3025 Parkview Drive, Hamel, MN 55340
Baker Chalet: (612) 473-4114
Hennepin Parks Administration Office, general information for all parks: (612) 559-9000
Reservations for lessons and programs: (612) 559-6700
TDD: (612) 559-6719
Trail conditions hotline for all parks: (612) 559-6778

5 Bald Eagle–Otter Lakes Regional Park
White Bear Lake, Minnesota

Trackset: 3 km　　　**Skating: 0 km**　　　**Ungroomed: 0 km**

Beginner, Intermediate, Advanced

Location

From St. Paul, north on I-35 for 7 miles, east on Minnesota Highway 96 for 1 mile, north on County Road 60 (Otter Lake Road) for 2 miles to the trailhead, on the west side of the road.

The park has two trail loops: beginner/intermediate and advanced. They skirt marshes, run through wooded and open areas, and around Fish and Tamarack lakes.

Ski equipment may be rented at Tamarack Nature Center from 9:00 a.m. to 5:00 p.m. on Monday through Saturday, and from noon to 5:00 p.m. on Sunday. Rental fees are $3.50 per hour with a minimum of two hours per rental. All equipment must be returned by 5:00 p.m. The Nature Center also offers many programs for adults and children. Many are free, but some require a small fee and/or reservations.

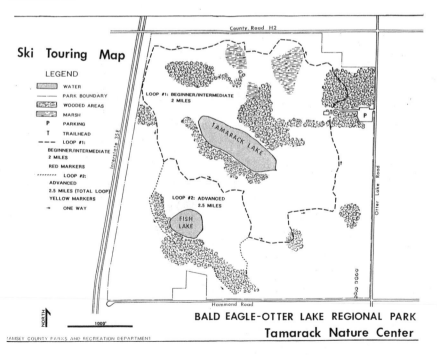

Contact
Tamarack Nature Center, Bald Eagle–Otter Lakes Regional Park, 5287 Otter Lake Road, White Bear Lake, MN 55110
(612) 429-7787
Ramsey County Parks and Recreation Department, 2015 North Van Dyke Street, Maplewood, MN 55109
(612) 777-1707

6 | Balsam Branch Trail
Balsam Lake, Wisconsin

Trackset: 0 km   **Skating: 0 km**   **Ungroomed: 5 km**

Beginner, Intermediate, Advanced

Location
From Taylors Falls, Minnesota, east on U.S. Highway 8 for 8 miles, 1 mile past intersection with Wisconsin Highway 65 turn south on County Road for 1 mile, east on County Road for 1 mile, south on County Road for .5 mile to the parking lot.

The Balsam Branch Trail has three loops: easy, intermediate, and advanced. They are interconnected, with the advanced loop farthest from the trailhead. The trails open December 1. They are not groomed, but the parking lot is plowed.

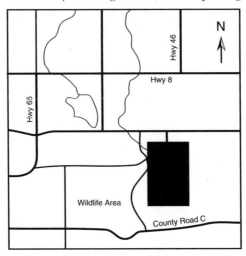

Contact
Polk County Parks, Box 623, Balsam Lake, WI 54810
(715) 485-3161

7 | Battle Creek Regional Park
St. Paul, Minnesota

Trackset: 8 km   **Skating: 1.5 km**   **Ungroomed: 0 km**

Beginner, Intermediate, Advanced

Location

Southeast corner of St. Paul and southern end of Maplewood. The park is divided into two sections. One entrance is on the west side of Winthrop Street, one block south of Upper Afton Road. The other entrance is on the north side of Lower Afton Road, one block east of McKnight Road.

The park is named for the Battle of Kaposia, a Native American battle waged in 1842. An Ojibwa band hid here in the deep gullies before attacking the Dakota village of Kaposia, across the Mississippi River on land that is now South St. Paul. Kaposia was the home of the Dakotah chieftains called Little Crow.

The two-loop trail at the Winthrop Street entrance is situated in hilly terrain, forested primarily with upland hardwoods such as maple and oak. The hills range from gentle to quite steep. This section, of intermediate difficulty, offers packed trails for skating. The network of trails at the Lower Afton Road entrance vary from beginner to advanced. These trails, for classic skiing only, run along ponds and through hills and meadows.

Ski equipment may be rented at Tamarack Nature Center (see entry 5: Bald Eagle-Otter Lakes Regional Park): from 9:00 a.m. to 5:00 p.m. on Monday through Saturday, and from noon to 5:00 p.m. on Sunday. Rental fees are $3.50 per hour with a minimum of two hours per rental. All equipment must be returned by 5:00 p.m. The Nature Center also offers many programs for adults and children. Many are free, but some require a small fee and/or reservations.

Contact

Ramsey County Parks and Recreation Department, 2015 North Van Dyke Street, Maplewood, MN 55109
(612) 777-1707

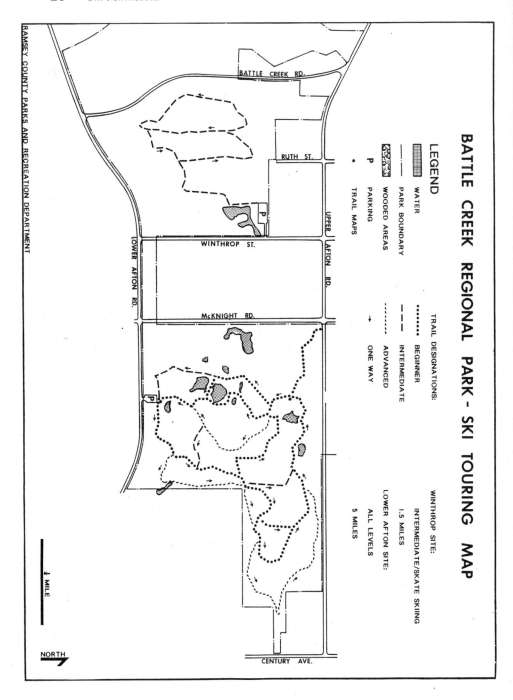

8 | Baylor Regional Park
Young America, Minnesota

Trackset: 5 km **Skating: 0 km** **Ungroomed: 0 km**

Beginner, Intermediate, Advanced

Location
From Young America, north on County Road 33 for 2.5 miles to the entrance, on the west side of the road.

The park, purchased by Carver County in 1971 with help from federal and state government, has wooded lake shore, rolling open land, forest, and marshes and other wetlands. Three-fourths of the park area is being maintained as a preserve in its natural state.

The trail loops begin at the park headquarters, a barn that houses the Carver County Historical Society's agricultural museum on its upper floor. The downstairs activity room includes kitchen facilities, comfortable furniture, restrooms, and showers. A group room may be reserved in advance. Ski equipment rental costs $1.50 per hour. The park is open 8:00 a.m. to 9:00 p.m.

Vehicles must have a permit: daily, $3; annual, $14; and senior citizen annual, $7.

Contact
Carver County Parks, 10775 County Road 33, Young America, MN 55397
Metro: 361-1000
Local: (612) 467-3145

Map following page

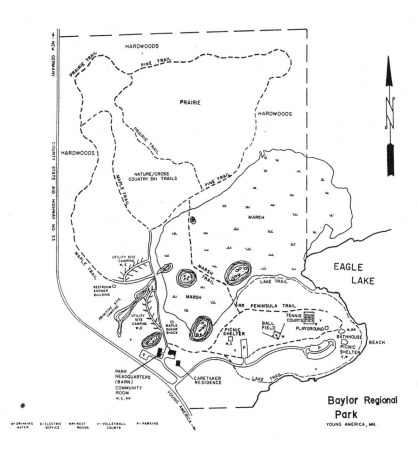

Baylor Regional
Park
YOUNG AMERICA, MN.

9 Big Willow Park
Minnetonka, Minnesota

Trackset: 1.6 km   **Skating: 0 km**   **Ungroomed: 0 km**

Beginner

Location

From Minneapolis, west on County Road 5 (Minnetonka Boulevard) for 5 miles to .5 mile west of the intersection with County Road 73. Parking is available near the ballfields, on the north side of the road.

The trail system is composed of two one-way loops and a connecting two-way trail. These easy trails run from the playing fields in the eastern end of the park to a small bridge in the western end. There are no facilities for skiers here.

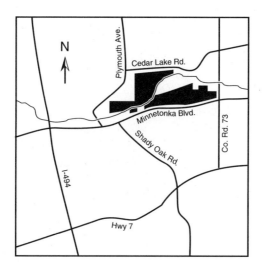

Contact

Minnetonka City Hall, Department of Parks and Recreation, 14600 Minnetonka Boulevard, Minnetonka, MN 55343
(612) 933-2511

10 | Birnamwood Park
Burnsville, Minnesota

Trackset: 1.3 km   **Skating: 0 km**   **Ungroomed: 0 km**

Beginner

Location

From I-35W, east on Burnsville Parkway for 2 miles, north on Parkwood Drive for
.5 mile to the trailhead, on the west side of the road.

There are two one-way loops of beginner-level trails connected by a two-way trail
that passes under Parkwood Drive. The chalet has concessions and restrooms.

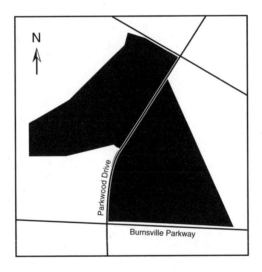

Contact

Burnsville Parks and Recreation, 100 Civic Center Pkwy, Burnsville, MN 55337
(612) 895-4500
Chalet: (612) 890-7964

11 Brackett's Crossing
Lakeville, Minnesota

Trackset: 25 km   **Skating: 0 km**   **Ungroomed: 0 km**

Beginner, Intermediate, Advanced

Location
From Burnsville, south on I-35 for 3 miles, west on 185th Street for 1 mile, north on Judicial Road for .5 mile to the entrance.

This country club, named after Lakeville's first settler, J. J. Brackett, is in a beautiful rural setting of heavily wooded rolling hills.

The trails begin at the clubhouse and are marked and fully groomed. Some have a single track, but many have two or even four four sets of tracks. They wind around many small ponds throughout the golf course and offer something to every type of skier.

The clubhouse is fully equipped with a sauna, showers, a complete restaurant and a ski shop for rental equipment. There is a $2.00 trail fee for guests; there is no parking fee. The hours for skiing are 10:00 a.m. to 5:00 p.m. on Saturday and Sunday.

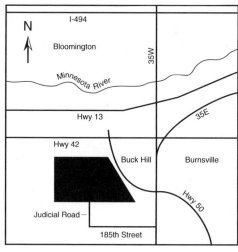

Contact
Brackett's Crossing, 17976 Judicial Road, Lakeville, MN 55044
Office: (612) 435-7600
Pro shop: (612) 435-7700

12 Bray Park
Madison Lake, Minnesota

Trackset: 4.8 km   **Skating: 0 km**   **Ungroomed: 0 km**

Beginner, Intermediate

Location
From the city of Madison Lake, east on Minnesota Highway 60 for 2 miles, south on County Road 48 for 2 miles to the park entrance on the southeast shore of Madison Lake, on the west side of the road.

The ski trails, a series of loops along the shores of Madison Lake, run through wooded and open areas. One trail features interpretive stations along the way. A side trail crosses a 70-foot swinging bridge over a deep ravine.

The facilities at the park include an interpretive center, picnic shelter, drinking water, and restrooms.

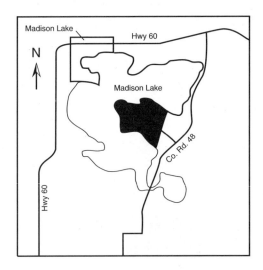

Contact
Blue Earth County Information Office, 204 South 5th Street, Mankato, MN 56001
(507) 389-8284

13 Bunker Hills Park
Coon Rapids, Minnesota

Trackset: 29 km   **Skating: 22 km**   **Ungroomed: 0 km**

Beginner, Intermediate, Advanced

Location
In Coon Rapids, from Minnesota Highway 242 (Main Street), north on County Road 11 (Foley Boulevard) for .5 mile to the parking lots at the golf course, archery range, or Bunker Lake.

Named for an early homesteader in Anoka County, this park is situated on a sand plain that was deposited during the retreat of Glacial Lake Grantsburg 10,000 years ago.

The trails are arranged in a system of interconnected one-way loops, and wind through beautiful woodlands forested with deciduous and coniferous trees and sand plain grasslands.The trails are thoroughly marked and color coded. The archery range loop is advanced; the other trails range from beginner to intermediate.

Shelters and toilets are scattered throughout the system. Maps, food, and equipment rentals are available at the clubhouse. The trails are open from 7:30 a.m. to 9:30 p.m. on every day of sufficient snow cover.

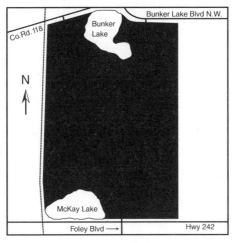

Contact
Anoka County Activities Center, 631 Main Street NW, Coon Rapids, MN 55433
(612) 757-3290

14 Cannon Valley Trail
Cannon Falls, Minnesota
to Red Wing, Minnesota

Trackset: 32 km   **Skating: 32 km**   **Ungroomed: 0 km**

Beginner

Location

In Cannon Falls there are several access points marked by signs just east of downtown. In Red Wing, access is from Old West Main Street, .5 mile west of Red Wing Pottery and Nybo's Landing.

The trail runs from Cannon Falls to Red Wing, along the Cannon River valley and past the town of Welch. Following the grade of a former Chicago Great Western Railroad line and close to the Cannon River, the trail affords spectacular views of the river and valley. The western half of the trail is characterized by high bluffs along the river and frequent sandstone and limestone outcrops; on the eastern half the river valley is wider and less steep. Most of the trail is heavily forested and high trees often overhang the trail from both sides.

The trail is open daily from sunrise until 10:00 p.m. It is regularly groomed and trackset for two-way travel, and skaters are welcome. No pets, horses, or motorized vehicles are allowed on the trail. Restrooms, telephones, food, and water are available in the three towns, and toilets are scattered along the trail.

Contact

City Hall, 306 West Mill Street, Cannon Falls, MN 55009
(507) 263-3954
Red Wing Area Chamber of Commerce, 420 Levee Street, Red Wing, MN 55066
(612) 388-4719
Welch Station: (612) 258-4141 (for a recorded message on current ski conditions)

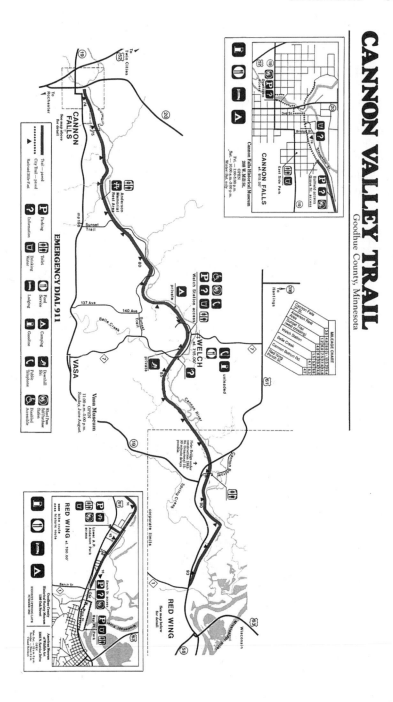

CANNON VALLEY TRAIL

Goodhue County, Minnesota

15 Carleton College Arboretum
Northfield, Minnesota

Trackset: 20 km   **Skating: 20 km**   **Ungroomed: 2 km**

Beginner, Intermediate

Location

From Northfield, northeast on Minnesota Highway 19 for .5 mile to the parking lot on the west side of the road.

The Carleton College Arboretum, or Arb, as students call it, is 450 acres of land to the north of the college. It is divided into two sections: the Lower and Upper Arboretum. The trailhead leads directly into the Lower Arboretum; the upper section is reached by skiing through a snow-packed tunnel under Highway 19.

The lower section is bordered on the west and north by the Cannon River. In the southern loops, trails run through the floodplain forest in the river valley. The northern trails wind through hardwood forest, huge tracts of prairie restoration, and mixed pine woods above the river valley. Although trails are beginner to intermediate, a few hills keep skiers on their toes. There is a good chance of seeing deer, rabbits, owls, and other wildlife, particularly at sunrise and sunset.

The Upper Arboretum is smaller than the lower section. Its trails run through

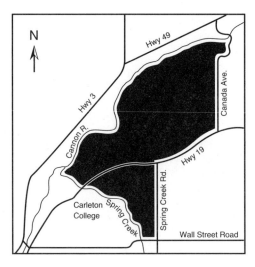

hardwood and softwood forests, prairie restoration areas, and around soccer and ultimate Frisbee fields.

No facilities are available at the trailhead. Maps can be purchased for $0.75 at the Carleton College Bookstore, which is located in Sayles-Hill Campus Center. The bookstore's hours are from 8:30 a.m. to 5:00 p.m. on Monday through Friday and from 10:00 a.m. to 2:00 p.m. on Saturday. Food and restrooms are available at the college and in Northfield.

Contact
Carleton College, 300 North College Street, Northfield, MN 55057
(507) 663-4000

16 Carver Park Reserve
Victoria, Minnesota

Trackset: 20.5 km   Skating: 6 km   Ungroomed: 0 km

Beginner, Intermediate, Advanced

Location
In Victoria, from Minnesota Highway 5, northwest on County Road 11 for 1 mile to the trailhead, on the west side of the road.

The trails wind through woods of basswood and maple and across marshlands. They skirt several lakes and the Fred E. King Waterfowl Sanctuary. The hilly terrain makes for delightful skiing. Although two short loops by the trailhead may be skied by novices, the other trails are intermediate to advanced.

The bulk of the trail system lies to the west of County Road 11, but the Nature Center Trail crosses the road, traverses the narrows of Crosby Lake, and eventually arrives at Lowry Nature Center. This year-round outdoor learning center conducts programs on various topics for groups and the general public every weekend. The center also has interesting displays, dining rooms, classrooms, laboratories, a library, and a bookstore. A large deer population can be observed at the feeders behind the Nature Center in the late afternoon. A visit to the Lowry Nature Center provides a welcome rest and greatly enhances a day of skiing.

Equipment may be rented at the trailhead, from 9:00 a.m. to 5:00 p.m. on weekends only, when ski trails are open.

Hennepin County Parks General Information
Trails are open from 8:00 a.m. to sunset. Some parks designate certain nights for moonlight or lantern skiing. All trails and accesses are open on holidays; however, trailheads, visitor centers, and other facilities close early or do not open on Thanksgiving Day, Christmas Eve, and Christmas Day.

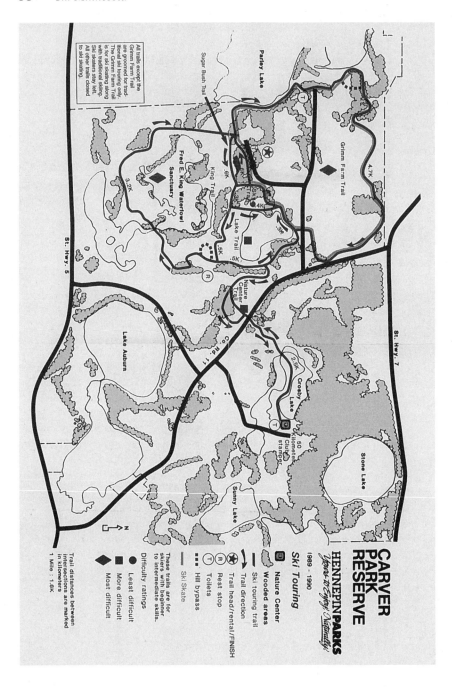

Many of the parks offer a full progression of ski lessons for children and adults, including instruction in classic and skating. To rent skis, boots, and poles, a picture ID is required. In addition to on-the-trail lessons, several indoor programs teach a variety of skiing basics, including an introduction to cross-country skiing, ski skating, telemark skiing, and ski waxing. There are also many non-skiing programs, such as snowshoeing and deer watching, for children and adults.

A parking fee is charged at all parks: daily, $4; annual, $20; senior citizens annual, $13. The first Tuesday of each month is a free day in all parks: no parking fees are charged. When a holiday falls on the first Tuesday of a month, the second Tuesday is a free day. Hennepin Parks permits are honored at Washington, Anoka, and Carver county parks. Washington and Anoka county parks permits are valid at Hennepin Parks facilities. When displayed with a $4 "Star" permit, Carver County permits are valid at Hennepin Parks.

The parks have a few simple rules:
- Ski during park operating hours only.
- Ski only on groomed trails and follow all directional signs.
- Dogs are not permitted on the ski trails.
- Ski trails are designed and maintained for skiing only. Hiking, sledding, snowshoeing, and snowmobiling can ruin a good ski track.

Contact
Hennepin Parks, 8737 East Bush Lake Road, Minneapolis, MN 55438
Trailhead: (612) 446-1801
Lowry Nature Center: (612) 472-4911
Hennepin Parks Administration Office, general information for all parks: (612) 559-9000
Reservations for lessons and programs: (612) 559-6700
TDD: (612) 559-6719
Trail conditions hotline for all parks: (612) 559-6778

17 Central Park–Nine Mile Creek Trail Bloomington, Minnesota

Trackset: 0 km   **Skating: 0 km**   **Ungroomed: 7.1 km**

Beginner, Intermediate, Advanced

Location
From Minneapolis, south on I-35W for 5 miles, west on Old Shakopee Road for 1 mile to the Moir Park trailhead, on the south side of the road.

Nine Mile Creek derived its name in Minnesota's earliest days because its confluence with the Minnesota River is nine miles from Fort Snelling.

The trail follows Nine Mile Creek from Moir Park to the Minnesota River bottom. The terrain involves gradual hills forested with hardwoods. There are, however, several steep, fast runs into the ravines of the river and creek bottoms. The trail is not groomed, but it is marked. Water, heated shelter, toilets, and ample parking are available during daylight hours at the Moir picnic grounds.

The trail connects with the Mound Springs Park Trail System at the river bottom.

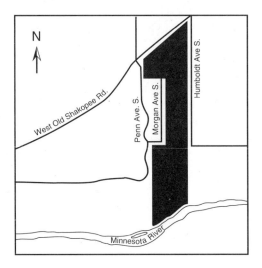

Contact
City of Bloomington, Parks and Recreation Division, 2215 West Old Shakopee Road, Bloomington, MN 55431
(612) 887-9638

18 Chomonix Cross-Country Ski Trails Lino Lakes, Minnesota

Trackset: 9 km **Skating: 2.5 km** **Ungroomed: 0 km**

Beginner, Intermediate

Location

In Lino Lakes, from I-35W, south on Minnesota Highway 49 (Lake Drive) for 1 mile, east on Aqua Lane for 1 mile to the clubhouse.

The ski trails at Chomonix are laid out in two sections: on the longer section, north of the clubhouse, only classic skiing is allowed. It runs north through the golf course and between Marshan and George Watch lakes. The southern loop, somewhat shorter, stays within the golf course.

Permits are required to use the trails. A season ticket costs $5 for an individual or $4 for each member in a family when purchased together. Daily passes are $2 for adults and $1.50 for children. Equipment may be rented at the clubhouse.

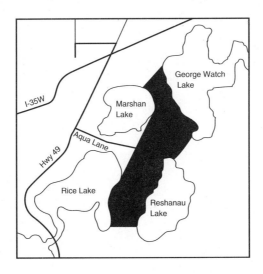

Contact

Anoka County Parks: (612) 757-3920
For ski conditions, rental, and permit information: (612) 482-8484

19 Cleary Lake Regional Park Prior Lake, Minnesota

Trackset: 15.6 km   **Skating: 0 km**   **Ungroomed: 0 km**

Beginner, Intermediate

Location
From Burnsville, west on County Road 42 (150th Street) for 2 miles, south on County Road 27 (Texas Avenue) for 4 miles to the entrance, on the west side of the road.

Set on the south side of Cleary Lake, the trail network traverses a gently rolling landscape, skirting the lake and winding through the woods. The loop at the trailhead is for beginners, and the two outer loops are intermediate. Rest stops and shelters are located on the trails.

The heated visitor center at the trailhead offers maps, rental equipment, restrooms, and light snacks. A warm fire in the fireplace will lift your spirits before or after skiing. The visitor center is open 10:00 a.m. to 5:00 p.m. on weekdays and 9:00 a.m. to 5:00 p.m. on weekends.

Hennepin County Parks General Information
Trails are open from 8:00 a.m. to sunset. Some parks designate certain nights for moonlight or lantern skiing. All trails and accesses are open on holidays; however, trailheads, visitor centers, and other facilities close early or do not open on Thanksgiving Day, Christmas Eve, and Christmas Day.

Many of the parks offer a full progression of ski lessons for children and adults, including instruction in classic and skating. To rent skis, boots, and poles, a picture ID is required. In addition to on-the-trail lessons, several indoor programs teach a variety of skiing basics, including an introduction to cross-country skiing, ski skating, telemark skiing, and ski waxing. There are also many non-skiing programs, such as snowshoeing and deer watching, for children and adults.

A parking fee is charged at all parks: daily, $4; annual, $20; senior citizens annual, $13. The first Tuesday of each month is a free day in all parks: no parking fees are charged. When a holiday falls on the first Tuesday of a month, the second Tuesday is a free day. Hennepin Parks permits are honored at Washington, Anoka, and Carver county parks. Washington and Anoka county parks permits are valid at Hennepin Parks facilities. When displayed with a $4 "Star" permit, Carver County permits are valid at Hennepin Parks.

The parks have a few simple rules:
- Ski during park operating hours only.
- Ski only on groomed trails and follow all directional signs.
- Dogs are not permitted on the ski trails.

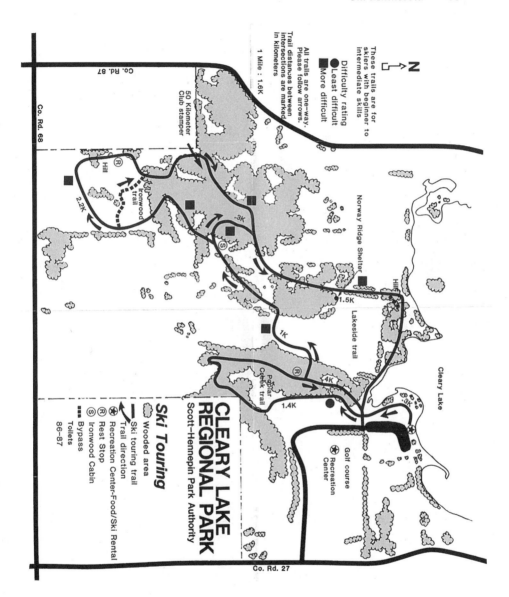

CLEARY LAKE REGIONAL PARK
Scott-Hennepin Park Authority

Ski Touring

- (wooded) Wooded area
- Ski touring trail
- ↗ Trail direction
- Ⓧ Recreation Center-Food/Ski Rental
- Ⓡ Rest Stop
- Ⓢ Ironwood Cabin
- ■■■ Bypass
- Toilets
- 86–87

These trails are for skiers with beginner to intermediate skills

Difficulty rating
● Least difficult
■ More difficult

All trails are one-way. Please follow arrows. Trail distances between intersections are marked in kilometers.

1 Mile : 1.6K

N →

Co. Rd. 87

Co. Rd. 68

Co. Rd. 27

50 Kilometer Club stamper

Ironwood trail

2.2K

Hill

.3K

1.5K

Hill

Norway Ridge Shelter

Lakeside trail

1K

Poplar Creek trail

1.4K

.4K

.3K

Cleary Lake

Golf course

Ⓧ Recreation Center

• Ski trails are designed and maintained for skiing only. Hiking, sledding, snow-shoeing, and snowmobiling can ruin a good ski track.

Contact
Hennepin Parks, 12615 County Road 9, Minneapolis, MN 55447
Visitor Center: (612) 447-2171
Baker Chalet: (612) 473-4114
Hennepin Parks Administration Office, general information for all parks: (612) 559-9000
Reservations for lessons and programs: (612) 559-6700
TDD: (612) 559-6719
Trail conditions hotline for all parks: (612) 559-6778

20 Collinwood Regional Park
Stockholm, Minnesota

Trackset: 4.8 km   Skating: 0 km   Ungroomed: 0 km

Beginner, Intermediate, Advanced

Location
From Minneapolis, west on U.S. Highway 12 for 38 miles to Cokato, south on County Road 3 for 3 miles, west on County Road 30 for 3 miles to the park entrance, on the south side of the road.

The trail system is set between Little Lake and Collinwood Lake. Most of the trails are rated for beginners, but a couple of sections are at the intermediate level, and a few steep hills challenge advanced skiers.

Facilities at the park include a picnic area with a shelter and toilets.

Contact
Wright County Parks Department, 3554 Braddock Avenue Northeast, Buffalo,
MN 55313
Local: (612) 682-7693
Metro: 339-6881
Toll-free: (800) 362-3667
Park manager: (612) 286-2801

21 Columbia Park
Minneapolis, Minnesota

Trackset: 2 km   **Skating: 0 km**   **Ungroomed: 0 km**

Beginner, Intermediate, Advanced

Location
From I-694, south on Minnesota Highway 65 (Central Avenue Northeast) for 2.5
miles to 33rd Street and the park entrance, on the west side of the road.

The trails are marked and groomed. The heated chalet has restrooms, food, and
equipment rentals. Columbia is open Saturday and Sunday, from 10:00 a.m. to
6:00 p.m., with expanded hours over the holiday season.

Contact
Columbia Park, 33rd Street and Central Avenue Northeast, Minneapolis,
MN 55418
(612) 789-2627
Minneapolis Parks and Recreation, 1301 Theodore Wirth Parkway, Minneapolis,
MN 55422
(612) 522-4584

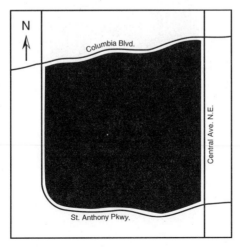

22 Como Ski Center
St. Paul, Minnesota

Trackset: 7 km   **Skating: 7 km**   **Ungroomed: 0 km**

Beginner

Location
In Saint Paul, from I-94, north on Lexington Parkway for 2 miles to the entrance to Como Park, on the west side of the road.

Two groomed trails run along the golf course and along the zoo. Como hosts several races, so the trails may be laid out in different routes from week to week. A 3 km loop of trail is lit for night skiing until 10:00 p.m. Equipment is available for rent, and beginner, intermediate, and skating lessons are offered, individually or in groups, with or without equipment. There are time trials every Thursday evening at 7:00 p.m. for a $2 fee.

The chalet, a warm retreat with restrooms and concessions, is open from 2:00 p.m. to 9:00 p.m. Monday through Friday, 9:00 a.m. to 6:00 p.m. Saturday, and 11:00 a.m. to 6:00 p.m. Sunday. Hours during holidays and school vacations depart from this schedule slightly.

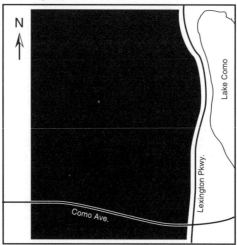

Contact
Como Golf Course, 1431 North Lexington Parkway, St. Paul, MN 55108
(612) 488-9673
City of Saint Paul, Division of Parks and Recreation, 25 West 4th Street, Room 300, St. Paul, MN 55102
(612) 292-7400

23 Coon Lake Trail
Frederic, Wisconsin

Trackset: 14 km   **Skating: 14 km**   **Ungroomed: 0 km**

Beginner, Intermediate, Advanced

Location
From Taylors Falls, Minnesota, east on U.S. Highway 8 for 4 miles, north on Wisconsin Highway 35 for 21 miles to Frederic, east on Ash Street for 6 blocks to the parking lot, on the north side of the road.

The trail has several one-way loops that vary in difficulty from beginner to advanced. They wind through pine forests along Coon Lake and through the lowlands of a stream at the northeast end of the lake. The trails are groomed weekly.

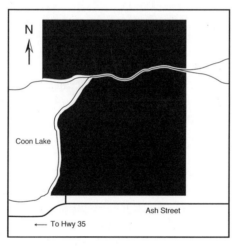

Contact
Frederick Area Community Association, P.O. Box 250, Frederick, WI 54837
(715) 327-4836
For trail conditions: (715) 327-4294

24 Cottage Grove Ravine Regional Park
Cottage Grove, Minnesota

Trackset: 11.3 km   Skating: 2.9 km   Ungroomed: 0 km

Beginner, Intermediate, Advanced

Location

From St. Paul, southeast on U.S. Highway 61 for 8 miles, north on County Road 19A (Chemolite Road) for .1 mile, east on the frontage road for .5 mile to the entrance gate, on the north side of the road.

The trails run through a four-mile ravine that provides 150 feet of elevation changes. The ravine is wooded, with scattered clearings of old field and meadow. The ravine and the land above were once prairie. Look for a variety of wildlife as you ski the trails.

There are two trailheads. The first leads from the access road to a short intermediate-to-advanced loop. The second trailhead, at the end of the access road, leads to the bulk of the trails, arranged in a series of connected loops. The first loop circles a pond and is suited to the novice. Intermediate and advanced loops branch off from this loop and travel northward for nearly the length of the park.

The shelter near the main parking lot provides trail maps, picnic tables, a fireplace and firewood, a serving counter, and restrooms.

Washington County Parks General Information

A parking permit, required for all vehicles entering Washington County parks, may be purchased at the Public Works Department, Lake Elmo Park Reserve, City of Cottage Grove, Forest Lake and Woodbury License Centers, and the Auditor-Treasurer's Office in the Stillwater Government Center. From June through August, permits are available at Square Lake Park and Cottage Grove Ravine Regional Park. Washington County permits are honored in Anoka, Carver, and Hennepin Parks.

The parks have a few simple rules:
- Skiing hours are from 7:00 a.m. to 30 minutes after sunset.
- Snowmobiling, hiking, sledding, and snowshoeing are not allowed.
- Dogs are not permitted on the ski trails.
- Place litter in the park's waste containers.
- Set fires only in the fire rings or fireplaces.
- Obey the speed limits and park only in designated areas.
- Alcoholic beverages are not permitted in the parks.
- Follow one-way trails in the proper direction.
- Skating is permitted only on designated loops.

Contact
Washington County Parks Section, 1515 Keats Avenue North, Lake Elmo, MN 55042
(612) 731-3851

25 Crow-Hassan Park Reserve Hanover, Minnesota

Trackset: 17.6 km   **Skating: 10 km**   **Ungroomed: 0 km**

Intermediate, Advanced

Location
From the junction of I-94 and I-494, northwest on I-94 for 8 miles, south on County Road 150 for 1 mile, northwest on County Road 116 (Territorial Road) for 2 miles, west on Hassan Parkway for 1.5 miles to the park entrance.

Although some sections of one trail loop are for beginners, most of the trails are designed for skiers with intermediate to advanced skills. Many of the outer trails run along the bluffs of the Crow River, which forms the northwest border of the park. The panoramic views offered at several points are outstanding. The trails run mainly through woodlands bordering a restored prairie, the park's dominant feature. Rest stops, shelters, and toilets are provided at several points on the trails. There is one ski-in camping site.

The trailhead provides maps, a lounge area with a woodstove, restrooms, ski wax, and concessions.

Hennepin County Parks General Information
Trails are open from 8:00 a.m. to sunset. Some parks designate certain nights for moonlight or lantern skiing. All trails and accesses are open on holidays; however, trailheads, visitor centers, and other facilities close early or do not open on Thanksgiving Day, Christmas Eve, and Christmas Day.

Many of the parks offer a full progression of ski lessons for children and adults, including instruction in classic and skating. To rent skis, boots, and poles, a picture ID is required. In addition to on-the-trail lessons, several indoor programs teach a variety of skiing basics, including an introduction to cross-country skiing, ski skating, telemark skiing, and ski waxing. There are also many non-skiing programs, such as snowshoeing and deer watching, for children and adults.

A parking fee is charged at all parks: daily, $4; annual, $20; senior citizens annual, $13. The first Tuesday of each month is a free day in all parks: no parking fees are charged. When a holiday falls on the first Tuesday of a month, the second Tuesday is a free day. Hennepin Parks permits are honored at Washington,

Anoka, and Carver county parks. Washington and Anoka county parks permits are valid at Hennepin Parks facilities. When displayed with a $4 "Star" permit, Carver County permits are valid at Hennepin Parks.

The parks have a few simple rules:

- Ski during park operating hours only.
- Ski only on groomed trails and follow all directional signs.
- Dogs are not permitted on the ski trails.
- Ski trails are designed and maintained for skiing only. Hiking, sledding, snowshoeing, and snowmobiling can ruin a good ski track.

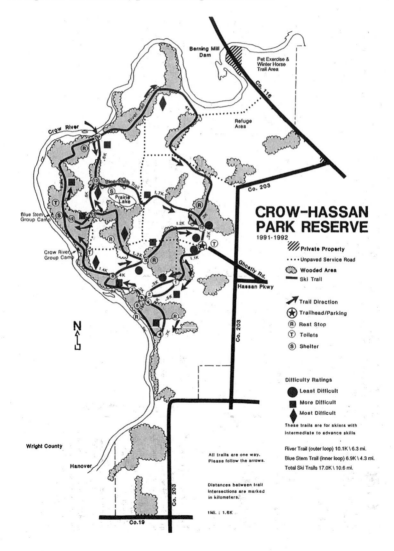

CROW–HASSAN PARK RESERVE

1991-1992

/// Private Property

• • • • Unpaved Service Road

Wooded Area

— Ski Trail

⬈ Trail Direction

★ Trailhead/Parking

Ⓡ Rest Stop

Ⓣ Toilets

Ⓢ Shelter

Difficulty Ratings

● Least Difficult

■ More Difficult

♦ Most Difficult

These trails are for skiers with intermediate to advance skills

River Trail (outer loop) 10.1K \ 6.3 mi.
Blue Stem Trail (inner loop) 6.9K \ 4.3 mi.
Total Ski Trails 17.0K \ 10.6 mi.

All trails are one way. Please follow the arrows.

Distances between trail intersections are marked in kilometers.

1 Mi. : 1.6K

Contact
Hennepin Parks, 13080 Territorial Road, Osseo, MN 55369
Trailhead: (612) 428-2765
Hennepin Parks Administration Office, general information for all parks:
(612) 559-9000
Reservations for lessons and programs: (612) 559-6700
TDD: (612) 559-6719
Trail conditions hotline for all parks: (612) 559-6778

26 East End Recreational Area
Red Wing, Minnesota

Trackset: 12.1 km **Skating: 5 km** **Ungroomed: 0 km**

Beginner, Intermediate, Advanced

Location
From St. Paul, southeast on U.S. Highway 61 for 15 miles, southeast on Minnesota Highway 316 for 10 miles, east on U.S. Highway 61 for 13 miles through downtown Red Wing and 1.5 miles past Barn Bluff, south on Golf Links Drive for .5 mile to the parking lot at Mississippi National Golf Links.

The trail system is comprised of four loops. The Memorial Park Trail, to the northwest of the trailhead is advanced, and the trails to the south and east of the trailhead are beginner and intermediate. The loop at the far eastern edge of the network is also designed for advanced skiers. The trails run through wooded, rolling terrain, passing open areas, and through the golf course. The clubhouse is open to skiers.

Contact
City of Red Wing, P.O. Box 34, Red Wing, MN 55066
(612) 388-6796

Map following page

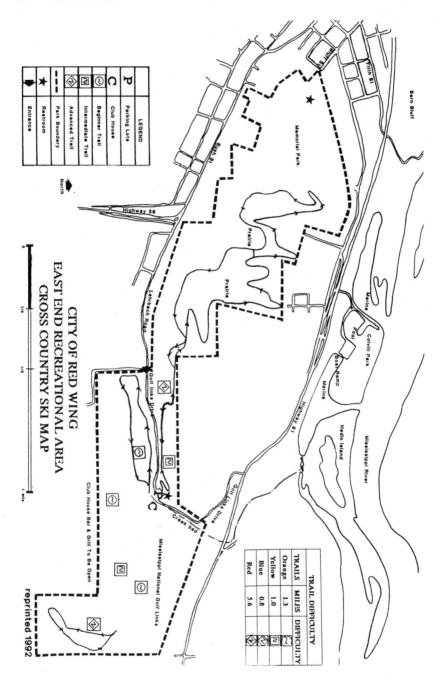

CITY OF RED WING
EAST END RECREATIONAL AREA
CROSS COUNTRY SKI MAP

reprinted 1992

LEGEND	
P	Parking Lots
C	Club House
①	Beginner Trail
②	Intermediate Trail
◈	Advanced Trail
- - -	Park Boundary
★	Restroom
➤	Entrance

North

0   1/4   1/2   1 mile

TRAIL DIFFICULTY			
TRAILS	MILES	DIFFICULTY	
Orange	1.3	◈	
Yellow	1.0	◈	
Blue	0.8	②	
Red	5.6	①	

Club House Bar & Grill To Be Open

Mississippi National Golf Links

Barn Bluff

Memorial Park

Prairie

Prairie

Bush St.

Highway 58

Lenbach Road

Golf links Drive

Golf Links Drive

Creek bed

Highway 61

Mississippi River

Hedin Island

Colvill Park

Marina

Boat Ramp

Pool

Marina

Fifth St.

S. Main

27 Elm Creek Park Reserve Maple Grove, Minnesota

Trackset: 14.7 km   Skating: 12.8 km   Ungroomed: 0 km

Beginner, Intermediate, Advanced

Location

From I-694, north on U.S. Highway 169 for 2 miles, west on County Road 81 for 3 miles, north on Territorial Road for 1 block to the park entrance, on the right side of the road.

Although the 1.4-km southern loop from the trailhead is rated as beginner, the remainder of the trails at the park are of intermediate or advanced difficulty. The woodlands of aspen, oak, maple, basswood, and birch shelter meadowlands, wetlands, lakes, and streams. A large intermediate loop circles Mud Lake, which, like the other lakes at Elm Creek, has a marshy shoreline that provides excellent habitat for waterfowl, beaver, deer, and countless other animals.

Near the confluence of Elm and Rush creeks, in the northwestern section of the park, is the Whitney H. Eastman Nature Center, a facility devoted to environmental education. It offers continuous outdoor, nature-oriented learning programs for schools as well as the general public. In addition, it serves as a beautiful visitor center and a pleasant place to warm up with a hot drink. The heated trail center, at the main trailhead, provides maps, rental equipment, light snacks, and restrooms.

Hennepin County Parks General Information

Trails are open from 8:00 a.m. to sunset. Some parks designate certain nights for moonlight or lantern skiing. All trails and accesses are open on holidays; however, trailheads, visitor centers, and other facilities close early or do not open on Thanksgiving Day, Christmas Eve, and Christmas Day.

Many of the parks offer a full progression of ski lessons for children and adults, including instruction in classic and skating. To rent skis, boots, and poles, a picture ID is required. In addition to on-the-trail lessons, several indoor programs teach a variety of skiing basics, including an introduction to cross-country skiing, ski skating, telemark skiing, and ski waxing. There are also many non-skiing programs, such as snowshoeing and deer watching, for children and adults.

A parking fee is charged at all parks: daily, $4; annual, $20; senior citizens annual, $13. The first Tuesday of each month is a free day in all parks: no parking fees are charged. When a holiday falls on the first Tuesday of a month, the second Tuesday is a free day. Hennepin Parks permits are honored at Washington, Anoka, and Carver county parks. Washington and Anoka county parks permits

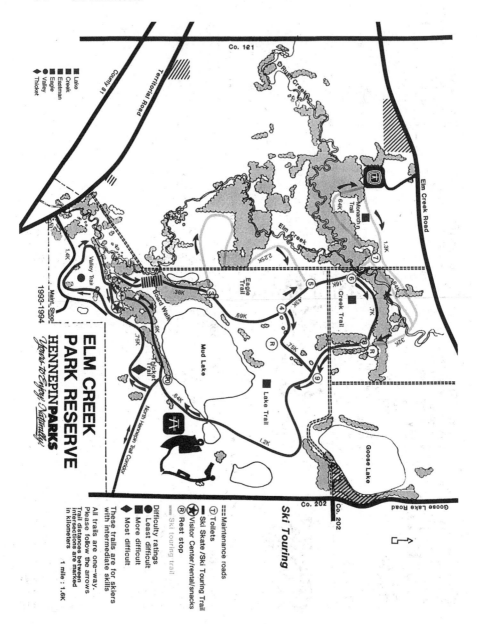

ELM CREEK PARK RESERVE

HENNEPIN PARKS

Yours to Enjoy Naturally

1993-1994

Maint. Shop

Ski Touring

=== Maintenance roads
(T) Toilets
🟢 Ski Skate/Ski Touring Trail
✪ Visitor Center/rental/snacks
(R) Rest stop
     Ski touring trail

Difficulty ratings
🔵 Least difficult
🟥 More difficult
◆ Most difficult

These trails are for skiers
with intermediate skills

All trails are one-way.
Please follow the arrows.
Trail distances between
intersections are marked
in kilometers.

1 mile : 1.6K

Lake
Creek
Eastman
Eagle
Valley
Thicket

County 81

Territorial Road

Co. 121

Rush Creek

Elm Creek Road

Elm Creek

Monarch Trail

.64K

1.3K

.225K

Eagle Trail

Valley Trail

Board Walk

.14K

.38K

.9K

.69K

.75K

Thicket Trail

Mud Lake

.64K

North Hennepin Trail Corridor

1.2K

Lake Trail

Creek Trail

.43K

.75K

.16K

7K

.54K

.32K

Goose Lake

Goose Lake Road

Co. 202

Co. 202

4

5

6

7

8

9

10

R

R

are valid at Hennepin Parks facilities. When displayed with a $4 "Star" permit, Carver County permits are valid at Hennepin Parks.

The parks have a few simple rules:
- Ski during park operating hours only.
- Ski only on groomed trails and follow all directional signs.
- Dogs are not permitted on the ski trails.
- Ski trails are designed and maintained for skiing only. Hiking, sledding, snow-shoeing, and snowmobiling can ruin a good ski track.

Contact

Hennepin Parks, 13080 Territorial Road, Osseo, MN 55369
Trailhead: (612) 424-5511
Eastman Nature Center: (612) 420-4300
Hennepin Parks Administration Office, general information for all parks: (612) 559-9000
Reservations for lessons and programs: (612) 559-6700
TDD: (612) 559-6719
Trail conditions hotline for all parks: (612) 559-6778

28 Fort Snelling State Park
St. Paul, Minnesota

Trackset: 26 km   **Skating: 6 km**   **Ungroomed: 0 km**

Beginner

Location

Near Minneapolis–St. Paul International Airport, on the Minnesota River at Post Road and Minnesota Highway 5. From I-35E, southwest on Minnesota Highway 5 for 2.5 miles; follow the signs to the parking lot.

Fort Snelling State Park is located at an enormously significant site in Minnesota's history: the confluence of the Mississippi and Minnesota rivers. The two rivers played an important role in the culture of the region as well. There can be no doubt that these rivers always had been significant to countless generations of Native Americans. The waterways also made it possible for Minnesota to open to white settlement. The Minnesota River flows from Big Stone Lake on the border between Minnesota and South Dakota; the Mississippi begins at Lake Itasca, in northern Minnesota. In the years before good roads were constructed, both rivers were important avenues for industry, commerce, and people. They are still used for such purposes today. Their confluence and attendant developments contributed greatly to the growth of St. Paul and Minneapolis.

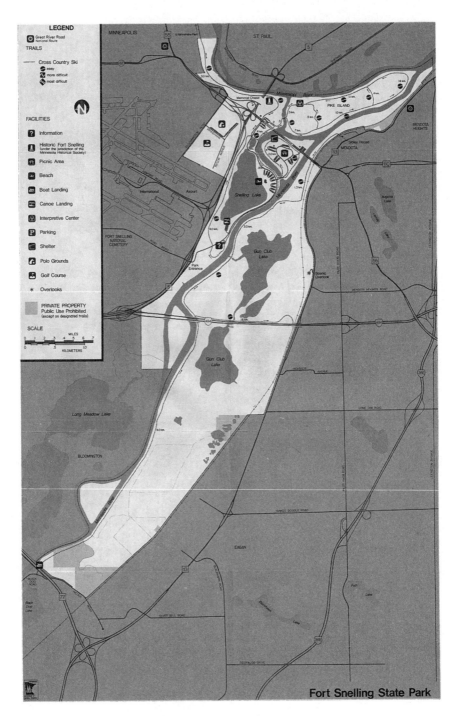

Fort Snelling State Park

Of course, the history of Fort Snelling receives emphasis in the park. The land was initially purchased in 1805 by Lieutenant Zebulon M. Pike, a famous military man and explorer, while on an expedition to discover the source of the Mississippi River. This purchase and the consequent establishment of the fort gave the United States control over the upper Mississippi. Construction of the fort began in 1819 under the command of Colonel Henry Leavenworth. In 1825, its name was changed from Fort St. Anthony to Fort Snelling, after its new commander, Colonel Josiah Snelling. The army at the fort served as a peacekeeper in conflicts between the Dakota and Ojibwa and the white traders and settlers. The fort remained a military post until 1946. In the 1960s the Minnesota Historical Society began a scrupulous restoration of the fort, and their efforts continue today.

The ski trails, used for hiking in warmer seasons, run through the forested river bottoms of cottonwood, green ash, elm, silver maple, and willow. They traverse land that is flat and smooth, which makes for easy skiing, and nearly ideal for moonlight skiing.

There are four basic, one-way trail systems. Pike Island Trail begins at the interpretive center and skirts the island's perimeter in a loop with two crossovers. This trail connects with Wood Duck Trail, which passes Snelling Lake, makes a circle on Picnic Island, and continues around Snelling Lake below the sandstone river bluffs. On this trail you may hear much airport and highway noise. The third trail, across the Minnesota River on the Dakota County side of the park, is the Mendota Trail, which follows an old settler trail through the river bottoms and traverses a major wildlife sanctuary. The main trailhead is near the historic Henry Sibley house in Mendota Heights, just northeast of the intersection of Minnesota highways 55 and 13. The fourth trail, the Minnehaha Trail, begins at the junction of Pike Island and Wood Duck trails. It follows on an old railroad grade along and above the Mississippi River, linking Fort Snelling, the Minneapolis trails system, and Minnehaha Park.

The interpretive center on Pike Island is host to a variety of year-round exhibits and programs that focus on the geology, wildlife, vegetation, and water resources of the park.

Minnesota State Parks General Information

- The parks are open year-round, but the hours vary.
- The use of weapons, traps, or nets is strictly prohibited.
- Pets must be kept on a leash no longer than six feet, and they are not allowed in the buildings or on the groomed ski trails.
- Motorized vehicles are permitted only on the park roads, not on the trails.
- Do not pick or dig up plants, disturb or feed animals, or scavenge dead wood.
- Daily or annual permits, required for all vehicles entering a state park, may be purchased at the park headquarters or the information center in St. Paul.

Contact
Fort Snelling State Park, Highway 5 and Post Road, St. Paul, MN 55111
(612) 725-2390
Department of Natural Resources, Division of Parks and Recreation,
500 Lafayette Road, St. Paul, MN 55155-4040
Metro: 296-6157
Non-metro: (800) 766-6000
TDD metro: 296-5484
TDD non-metro: (800) 657-3929

29 French Regional Park
Plymouth, Minnesota

Trackset: 8.7 km   Skating: 7.1 km   Ungroomed: 0 km

Beginner, Intermediate, Advanced

Location
From I-494, east on County Road 9 for less than 1 mile to the park entrance, on
the south side of the road.

The park's acreage is located around the northwest arm of Medicine Lake, a com-
plex system of bays, channels, narrows, and backwaters. The trailhead is on the
east central side of the park. Although short in length, French's trails offer something for every type of skier. The beginner's loop, to the southeast of the trailhead, passes through the park's most heavily wooded area, skirting the north side
of Medicine Lake and passing over channels fed by the main bay of the lake. The
loops for intermediate skiers, to the northwest of the trail center, lead to the west
side of the bay and to Challenge Hill and Skyline trails, both of which give good
workouts for intermediate and advanced skiers. The heights of these trails offer
spectacular views of the park, Medicine Lake, and the Minneapolis skyline. Even
though this is a fairly urban park, skiers can see signs of deer, beaver, and fox
along the trails. There are toilets and shelters along the trails. After sunset, over
6 km of trails are lit for night skiing until 9:00 p.m., weather permitting. The
sight of lights weaving through the woods can make night skiing one of the most
magical cross-country skiing experiences. The lights are not turned on for Christmas Eve or Christmas Day.
    The visitor center has a lounge with a fireplace and offers trail maps, rental
equipment, merchandise, food, and restrooms. There are also shelters and toilets
along the trails.

French Regional Park
HENNEPIN**PARKS**

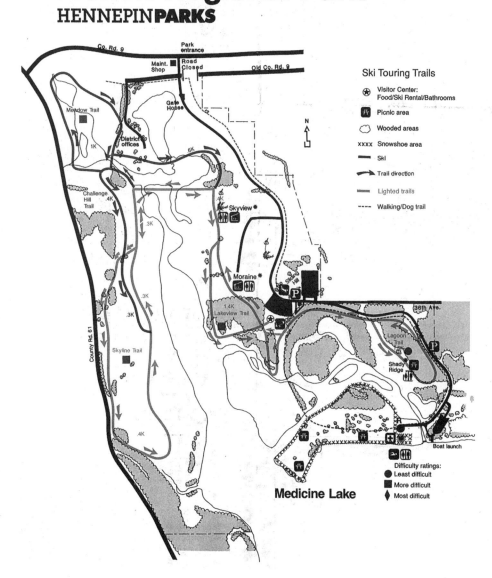

Ski Touring Trails

⊛ Visitor Center:
Food/Ski Rental/Bathrooms

Picnic area

Wooded areas

xxxx Snowshoe area

▬ Ski

Trail direction

Lighted trails

---- Walking/Dog trail

Difficulty ratings:
● Least difficult
■ More difficult
◆ Most difficult

Medicine Lake

Hennepin County Parks General Information

Trails are open from 8:00 a.m. to sunset. Some parks designate certain nights for moonlight or lantern skiing. All trails and accesses are open on holidays; however, trailheads, visitor centers, and other facilities close early or do not open on Thanksgiving Day, Christmas Eve, and Christmas Day.

Many of the parks offer a full progression of ski lessons for children and adults, including instruction in classic and skating. To rent skis, boots, and poles, a picture ID is required. In addition to on-the-trail lessons, several indoor programs teach a variety of skiing basics, including an introduction to cross-country skiing, ski skating, telemark skiing, and ski waxing. There are also many non-skiing programs, such as snowshoeing and deer watching, for children and adults.

A parking fee is charged at all parks: daily, $4; annual, $20; senior citizens annual, $13. The first Tuesday of each month is a free day in all parks: no parking fees are charged. When a holiday falls on the first Tuesday of a month, the second Tuesday is a free day. Hennepin Parks permits are honored at Washington, Anoka, and Carver county parks. Washington and Anoka county parks permits are valid at Hennepin Parks facilities. When displayed with a $4 "Star" permit, Carver County permits are valid at Hennepin Parks.

The parks have a few simple rules:

• Ski during park operating hours only.
• Ski only on groomed trails and follow all directional signs.
• Dogs are not permitted on the ski trails.
• Ski trails are designed and maintained for skiing only. Hiking, sledding, snowshoeing, and snowmobiling can ruin a good ski track.

Contact

Hennepin Parks, 8737 East Bush Lake Road, Minneapolis, MN 55438
Visitor Center: (612) 559-8891
Hennepin Parks Administration Office, general information for all parks: (612) 559-9000
Reservations for lessons and programs: (612) 559-6700
TDD: (612) 559-6719
Trail conditions hotline for all parks: (612) 559-6778

30 Frontenac State Park
Frontenac, Minnesota

Trackset: 10 km **Skating: 10 km** **Ungroomed: 0 km**

Beginner, Intermediate

Location

From Red Wing, southeast on U.S. Highway 61 for 10 miles, northeast on County Road 2 for 1 mile to the park gate, on the west side of the road. The park is on the western shore of Lake Pepin.

The high bluffs, deep valleys, and other characteristic landscape patterns which surround the park were sculpted to their present shape during the last glacial period, which ended more than 10,000 years ago. Meltwater from the last glacier formed Glacial Lake Agassiz, which was larger than the Great Lakes combined. From its southern end, Glacial River Warren flowed with high energy, cutting the large valley through which the Minnesota River now flows. It grew in strength from the meltwaters that were coursing through the valleys that presently hold the Mississippi and St. Croix rivers. This powerful water deeply eroded the limestone bedrock of southeastern Minnesota and shaped the Frontenac area as we see it today.

The Frontenac limestone is of the highest quality and was chosen in 1883 by architects LaFarge and Heins for the construction of the Cathedral of St. John the Divine in New York City.

The trail system encompasses landscape of tremendous variety. The northern loop, of intermediate difficulty, moves through hilly terrain atop and below the limestone bluffs overlooking Lake Pepin and the town of Frontenac. The southern trail, for beginners, skirts Old Frontenac and ends on Sand Point, along the river's edge. Snowmobiling is allowed at Frontenac. One snowmobile trail crosses the northernmost branch of the ski trail, but otherwise the two systems do not intersect. Maps and restrooms are available at the heated trail center. Winter camping is allowed.

Minnesota State Parks General Information

- The parks are open year-round, but the hours vary.
- The use of weapons, traps, or nets is strictly prohibited.
- Pets must be kept on a leash no longer than six feet, and they are not allowed in the buildings or on the groomed ski trails.
- Motorized vehicles are permitted only on the park roads, not on the trails.
- Do not pick or dig up plants, disturb or feed animals, or scavenge dead wood.
- Daily or annual permits, required for all vehicles entering a state park, may be purchased at the park headquarters or the information center in St. Paul.

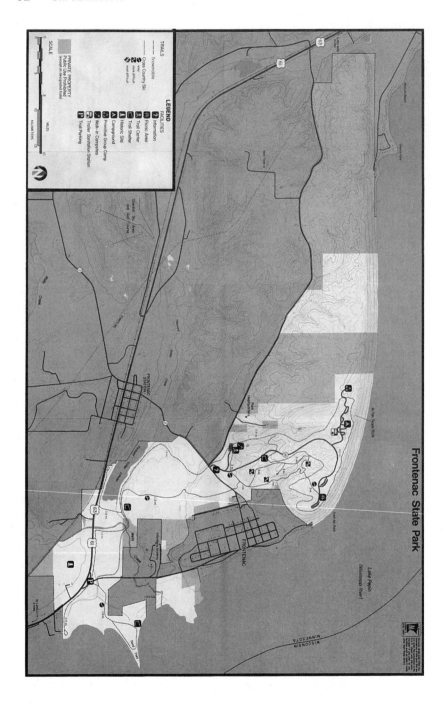

Contact

Frontenac State Park, Route 2, Box 134, Lake City, MN 55041
(612) 345-3401
Department of Natural Resources, Division of Parks and Recreation,
500 Lafayette Road, St. Paul, MN 55155-4040
Metro: 296-6157
Non-metro: (800) 766-6000
TDD metro: 296-5484
TDD non-metro: (800) 657-3929

31 | Gateway Trail
St. Paul to Pine Point Park

Trackset: 15.5 km   **Skating: 0 km**   **Ungroomed: 1.4 km**

Beginner

Location

Three entry points:

• In Oakdale, from the intersection of I-694 and Minnesota Highway 36, south
on Hadley Avenue for less than a block, east on 55th Street North for .5 mile to
the parking area, on the south side of the road.
• West of Stillwater, near the intersection of Minnesota Highway 96 and County
Road 63 (Kimbro Avenue North) is a trail parking lot.
• From Stillwater, north on County Road 55 for 5 miles to Pine Point Park. This
Washington County park has a small fee for parking (see entry 67).
• Parking is also permitted on some of the streets that cross the trail, but parked
cars must not obstruct the skiers' view of traffic.

The Gateway Trail, 16.9 miles long, is a multi-use recreational trail from northern St. Paul to Pine Point Park, near Stillwater. It is part of the Willard Munger State Trail, which is being developed from St. Paul to Duluth. Other segments of the Willard Munger State Trail run from Hinckley to Barnum, from Carleton to West Duluth on a former railroad grade, and through state parks and forests in eastern Minnesota.

Following a former Soo Line Railway grade, the Gateway Trail cuts through a variety of terrain, from urban neighborhoods through parks and suburbs, and out to the lakes, wetlands, fields, and wooded countryside of Washington County. Many trail users are surprised to find these rural landscapes so close to the Twin Cities.

Although the trail begins near Como and Phalen-Keller regional parks, the section of the trail groomed for cross-country skiing starts at the intersection of I-694 and Minnesota Highway 36. No motorized vehicles are allowed, and the trails for skiing and horseback riding are separate.

Contact

Department of Natural Resources, Division of Parks and Recreation, 500 Lafayette Road, St. Paul, MN 55155-4040
Metro: 296-6157
Non-metro: (800) 766-6000
TDD metro: 296-5484
TDD non-metro: (800) 657-3929

32 Girard Lake Park
Bloomington, Minnesota

Trackset: 0 km   **Skating: 0 km**   **Ungroomed: 1.7 km**

Beginner

Location

From the intersection of I-35W and I-494, west on I-494 for 1.5 miles, south on France Avenue South for .5 mile, east on West 84th Street for less than a mile to the trailhead, on the south side of the road.

The trail is a single loop around Girard Lake. It is ideal for families, because the terrain is very flat and easy for beginners. Although the trail is not groomed, it is well-marked. No facilities are available for skiers at this park.

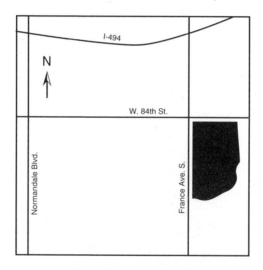

Contact

City of Bloomington, Parks and Recreation Division, 2215 West Old Shakopee Road, Bloomington, MN 55431
(612) 887-9638

33 Glen Hills County Park
Wilson, Wisconsin

Trackset: 6.4 km   Skating: 0 km   Ungroomed: 0 km

Beginner, Intermediate, Advanced

Location
From St. Paul, east on I-94 for 50 miles to the Glenwood City exit, north on Wisconsin Highway 128 for 4 miles, east on County Road E for 1 mile, north on Rustic Road 3 for 1.5 miles to the day-use entrance of the park, on the east side of the road.

Glen Hills Park, in the hill country of western Wisconsin, consists of 700 wooded acres surrounding Glen Lake. The well-signed ski trails are laid out in a series of connected loops, mostly moving through wooded areas. The trails along Glen Lake, to the south and west of the trailhead, are for beginners. The more difficult trails are north and west of the trail center.

Toilets are available at the trailhead. Daily or annual permits, required for all vehicles entering the park, cost $2 or $15 respectively and may be purchased at the park office or the self-registration station at the park entrance. Snowmobiles are allowed in the park but not on the ski trails.

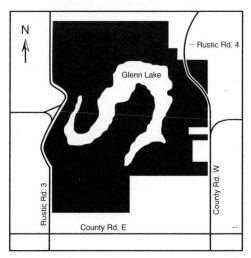

Contact
Glen Hills Park Manager, 1049 Rustic Road 3, Glenwood City, WI 54013
(715) 265-4613

34 | Grantsburg Nordic Ski Trail
Grantsburg, Wisconsin

Trackset: 11 km   **Skating: 11 km**   **Ungroomed: 0 km**

Intermediate, Advanced

Location

From St. Paul, north on I-35 for 45 miles, east on Minnesota Highway 70 for 11 miles to Grantsburg, north on Wisconsin Highway 48 for 5 blocks, west on Olson Drive for 4 blocks to the trailhead, on the north side of the road.

Called the "Big G" by many locals, this trail system offers great variety for skiers. The trails are a series of one-way loops and two-way connecting trails, running along Hay Creek and Wood River They incorporate many big hills and some human-made moguls and racetrack-style banked turns at the bottoms of hills. These advanced features can be avoided by following the many cutoffs and gentler runs around steep hills.

Contact

Village of Grantsburg, 416 South Pine Street, Grantsburg, WI 54840
(715) 463-2405

Map following page

Grantsburg Nordic Ski Trail

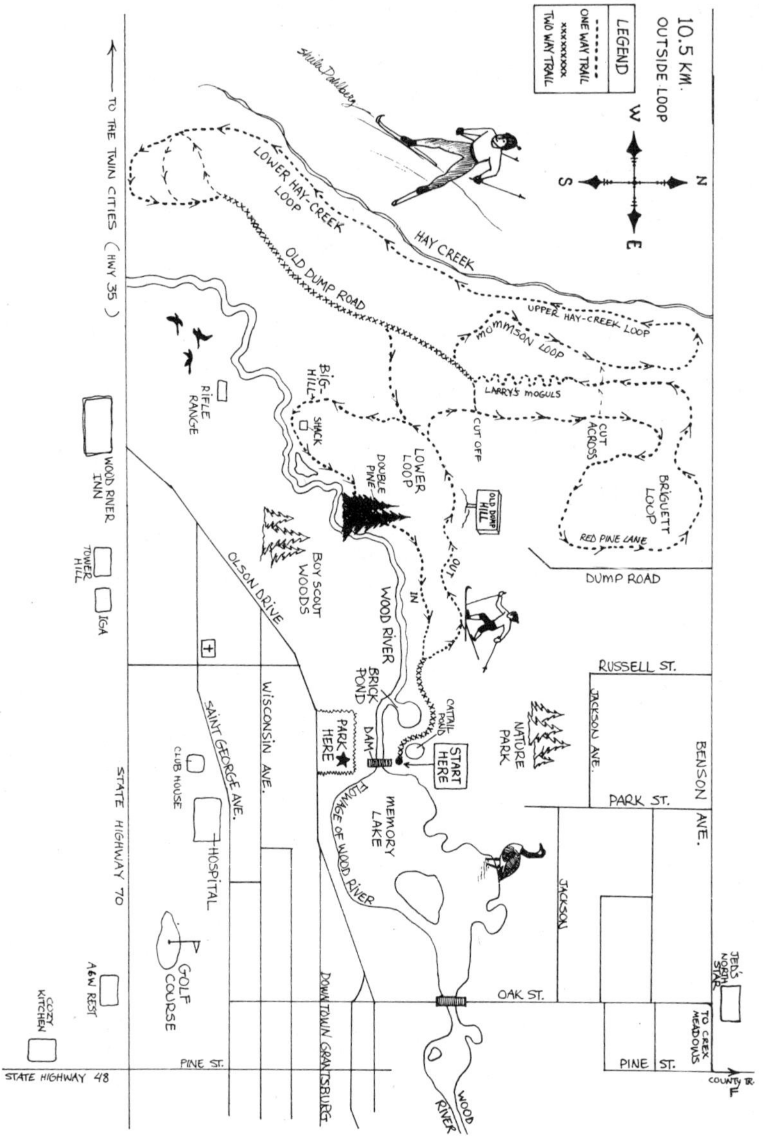

35 Harry Larson Memorial County Forest Silver Creek, Minnesota

Trackset: 3.6 km   **Skating: 0 km**   **Ungroomed: 0 km**

Beginner

Location
From Minneapolis, northwest on I-94 for 22 miles to Monticello, west on County Road 39 for 10 miles, north on County Road 111 for 5 miles to the park entrance, on the east side of the road.

From the trailhead, the ski trail moves to the northeast in two consecutive 1.8-km loops. The terrain involves rolling hills with a mature oak forest, some aspen, and pothole marshes.

The park provides a picnic area, drinking water, and toilets.

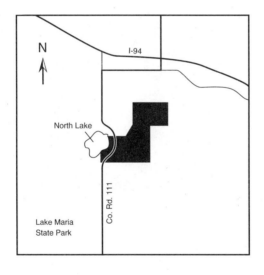

Contact
Wright County Parks Department, 3554 Braddock Avenue Northeast, Buffalo, MN 55313
Local: (612) 682-7693
Metro: 339-6881
Toll-free: (800) 362-3667

36 Hiawatha Golf Course
Minneapolis, Minnesota

Trackset: 2 km   Skating: 0 km   Ungroomed: 0 km

Beginner, Intermediate

Location

In southeastern Minneapolis, at Lake Hiawatha, at the intersection of West 46th Street and Longfellow Avenue South.

The ski trails are well marked and involve a flat terrain. Heated shelter, restrooms, food, and rental equipment are available when the facility is open, on Saturday and Sunday, 10:00 a.m. to 6:00 p.m., with expanded hours during the holiday season.

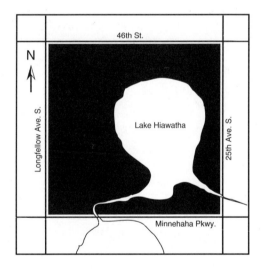

Contact

Hiawatha Golf Course, West 46th Street and Longfellow Avenue South, Minneapolis, MN 5540
(612) 724-7715
Minneapolis Parks and Recreation, 1301 Theodore Wirth Parkway, Minneapolis, MN 55422
(612) 522-4584

37 Hidden Falls–Crosby Farm Regional Park
St. Paul, Minnesota

Trackset: 13.9 km   **Skating: 0 km**   **Ungroomed: 0 km**

Beginner, Intermediate

Location

In southwestern St. Paul, with two entry points:

- From the St. Paul side of the Mississippi River at the West 7th Street Bridge (Minnesota Highway 5), east on Shepard Road for less than a mile to the parking lot, on the south side of the road.
- From the St. Paul side of the Mississippi River at the West 7th Street Bridge (Minnesota Highway 5), west and north on Mississippi River Boulevard for 1.5 miles to the park access road, on the west side of the street.

The trails run through the floodplain forest of the Mississippi River valley. In a series of loops and longer connecting trails, they pass Fort Snelling, the Watergate Marina, and Crosby Lake, all beneath spectacular 150-foot river bluffs.

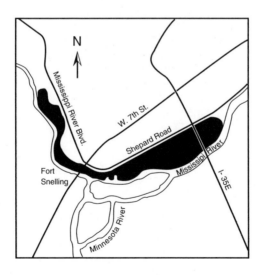

Contact

City of Saint Paul, Division of Parks and Recreation, 25 West 4th Street, Room 300, St. Paul, MN 55102
(612) 292-7400 or (612) 292-7445

38 Highland Nine-Hole Golf Course St. Paul, Minnesota

Trackset: 3 km   **Skating: 0 km**   **Ungroomed: 0 km**

Beginner

Location

In southwestern St. Paul, from I-94, south on Hamline Avenue for 2.5 miles to the entrance, on the west side of the road, just south of the intersection of Hamline and Montreal avenues.

The trails consist of two short loops, one inside the other, but may be groomed in a different manner from year to year. They cover the terrain of the golf course.

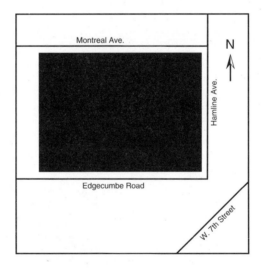

Contact

City of Saint Paul, Division of Parks and Recreation, 25 West 4th Street, Room 300, St. Paul, MN 55102
(612) 292-7400 or (612) 292-7445

39 Hyland Lake Park Reserve Bloomington, Minnesota

Trackset: 10.8 km   Skating: 10.8 km   Ungroomed: 0 km

Beginner, Intermediate, Advanced

Location

From I-494, south on County Road 34 (Normandale Boulevard) for .5 mile, west on West 84th Street for .5 mile, southwest on East Bush Lake Road for 2 miles, south on Bush Lake Road for .5 mile to the park entrance, on the east side of the road.

The reserve includes marshy lowlands, gently rolling meadows, lakes, and the Mount Gilboa highlands. The ski trails run through the southern two-thirds of the reserve. The three central loops have a gentle terrain suitable for the beginner, and the northern and southern loops challenge the advanced skier. The lighted Star Loop offers 1 km of night skiing on Friday and Saturday nights until 9:00 p.m. Other ski trails are open weekdays from 10:00 a.m. to 5:00 p.m. and weekends from 9:00 a.m. to 5:00 p.m.

All trails begin at the visitor center, which offers maps, rental equipment, concessions, merchandise, a lounge area, and restrooms. Lessons are also available.

Beyond the northern loop is the Hyland Hills Ski Area, which offers downhill skiing and ski jumping. Call (612) 835-4250 or (612) 835-4604 for further information.

Northwest of the northern loop is the trail to Richardson Nature Center, open daily from 9:00 a.m. to 5:00 p.m. The facility, devoted to environmental education for schools and the public, offers programs in outdoor learning throughout the year. It is fully equipped with laboratories, classrooms, and exhibits. Its main entrance is north of the park's entrance.

Hennepin County Parks General Information

Trails are open from 8:00 a.m. to sunset. Some parks designate certain nights for moonlight or lantern skiing. All trails and accesses are open on holidays; however, trailheads, visitor centers, and other facilities close early or do not open on Thanksgiving Day, Christmas Eve, and Christmas Day.

Many of the parks offer a full progression of ski lessons for children and adults, including instruction in classic and skating. To rent skis, boots, and poles, a picture ID is required. In addition to on-the-trail lessons, several indoor programs teach a variety of skiing basics, including an introduction to cross-country skiing, ski skating, telemark skiing, and ski waxing. There are also many non-skiing programs, such as snowshoeing and deer watching, for children and adults.

A parking fee is charged at all parks: daily, $4; annual, $20; senior citizens annual, $13. The first Tuesday of each month is a free day in all parks: no parking fees are charged. When a holiday falls on the first Tuesday of a month, the second Tuesday is a free day. Hennepin Parks permits are honored at Washington, Anoka, and Carver county parks. Washington and Anoka county parks permits are valid at Hennepin Parks facilities. When displayed with a $4 "Star" permit, Carver County permits are valid at Hennepin Parks.

The parks have a few simple rules:
- Ski during park operating hours only.
- Ski only on groomed trails and follow all directional signs.
- Dogs are not permitted on the ski trails.
- Ski trails are designed and maintained for skiing only. Hiking, sledding, snowshoeing, and snowmobiling can ruin a good ski track.

Contact
Hennepin Parks, 8737 East Bush Lake Road, Minneapolis, MN 55438
Visitor Center: (612) 941-4362
Richardson Nature Center: (612) 835-4250 or (612) 941-7993
Hennepin Parks Administration Office, general information for all parks: (612) 559-9000
Reservations for lessons and programs: (612) 559-6700
TDD: (612) 559-6719
Trail conditions hotline for all parks: (612) 559-6778

HYLAND LAKE PARK RESERVE

HENNEPIN PARKS
Yours to Enjoy Naturally!

W. 84th St.

Chalet Rd.

E. Bush Lk. Rd.

Nature Center Spur

.9K

.6K

9K

1.2K

North Trail
3.3K

.5K

.1K

.7K

Oak
Knob
Trail

1.0K

.4K

Star Loop Lighted trail

Parking

1.7K

.2K

.1K

Danger
Thin
Ice

.3K

Entrance

Lake Trail

.8K

Danger
Thin Ice

Hyland Lake

.9K

Hill Trail

1.0K

1.9K

Co. Rd. 28

Bush Lake Rd.

N

Ski Touring

Difficulty Ratings

● Least Difficult

■ More Difficult

◆ Most Difficult

These trails are for skiers with
beginner to intermediate skills.

Ski Jump

Hyland Hills

Richardson Nature Center

Visitor Center/Food
Ski Rental

Private Property

Wooded Areas

── Ski Skating/Ski Touring Trail

↘ Trail Direction

Ⓡ Rest Stop

Ⓣ Toilets

--- Dog Walking & Hiking Trail

All trails are one way
unless marked.
Please follow the arrows

Trail distances between
intersections are marked
in kilometers

1MI. : 1.6K

40 Interstate State Park
St. Croix Falls, Wisconsin

Trackset: 17.9 km   Skating: 0 km   Ungroomed: 0 km

Beginner, Intermediate, Advanced

Location

From Taylors Falls, Minnesota, east on U.S. Highway 8 for .5 mile, south on Wisconsin Highway 35 for .5 mile to the park entrance, on the west side of the road.

Interstate State Park is located in some of the most beautiful and atypical terrain in this part of the Midwest. More than a billion years ago, what is now the continent of North America began to split apart, along a line from northeast of Thunder Bay, Ontario to Nebraska and Kansas. The resultant rift valley allowed many flows of volcanic basalt to extrude from beneath the Earth's crust. This igneous rock has since been eroded and covered by many layers of sediment. Much more recently, glaciers covered much of what is now Minnesota. When the climate warmed and these massive sheets of ice retreated, an enormous disgorge of meltwater scoured out the St. Croix River valley, exposing the ancient volcanic rock and creating the spectacular river valley and jagged outcrops at Taylors Falls and St. Croix Falls.

Skiing in Interstate State Park is enjoyable for skiers of all ages and abilities. Most of the trails are for beginners, but intermediate and advanced skiers will find one suitable trail each. The trails move through sugar and silver maple forests, past beaver ponds and marshes, and along the bluffs of the St. Croix River and its tributary streams. Many rock outcrops are passed throughout the trail system. Skiers should be aware that not all trails are always groomed; the extent of grooming will vary from month to month. A warming shelter is located near the lower parking lot.

The Ice Age Interpretive Center, open daily from 8:00 a.m. to 4:30 p.m., has many exhibits and a film about the ice age and the local geology. Daily or annual Wisconsin State Park permits, required for all vehicles entering a state park, may be purchased at the park office.

Contact

Interstate State Park, Box 703, St. Croix Falls, WI 54024
(715) 483-3747

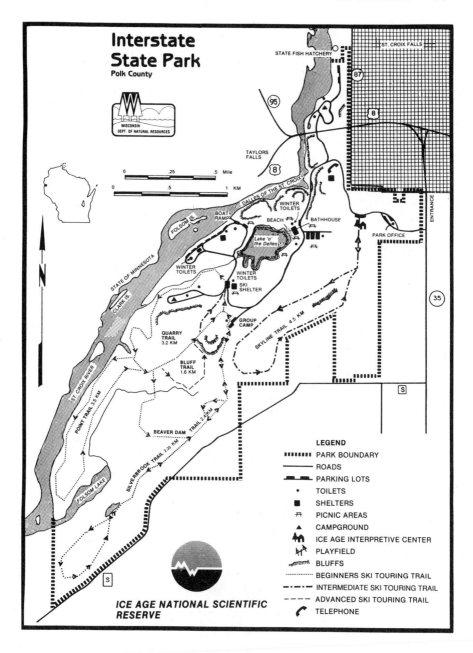

Interstate State Park
Polk County

WISCONSIN
DEPT. OF NATURAL RESOURCES

ST. CROIX FALLS

STATE FISH HATCHERY

87

95

8

TAYLORS
FALLS

8

DALLES OF THE ST. CROIX

WINTER
TOILETS

BOAT
RAMP

BEACH

BATHHOUSE

PARK OFFICE

ENTRANCE

*Lake 'o'
the Dalles*

35

STATE OF MINNESOTA

FOLSOM

WINTER
TOILETS

WINTER
TOILETS

SKI
SHELTER

CLARK IS.

GROUP
CAMP

SKYLINE TRAIL 4.5 KM

QUARRY
TRAIL
3.2 KM

BLUFF
TRAIL
1.6 KM

ST. CROIX RIVER

POINT TRAIL 3.5 KM

TRAIL 2.5 KM

BEAVER DAM

SILVERBROOK TRAIL 2.38 KM

S

FOLSOM LAKE

S

LEGEND

- ▬▬▬▬ PARK BOUNDARY
- ───── ROADS
- ▬▬▬ PARKING LOTS
- • TOILETS
- ■ SHELTERS
- ⌕ PICNIC AREAS
- ▲ CAMPGROUND
- ♣ ICE AGE INTERPRETIVE CENTER
- ⚘ PLAYFIELD
- ▱ BLUFFS
- ·········· BEGINNERS SKI TOURING TRAIL
- –·–·– INTERMEDIATE SKI TOURING TRAIL
- – – – ADVANCED SKI TOURING TRAIL
- ☎ TELEPHONE

*ICE AGE NATIONAL SCIENTIFIC
RESERVE*

0   .25   .5 Mile

0   .5   1 KM

N

41 | Kaplan's Woods Parkway Owatonna, Minnesota

Trackset: 13.5 km   Skating: 0 km   Ungroomed: 0 km

Beginner, Intermediate, Advanced

Location
From Minneapolis, south on I-35 for 60 miles, east on U.S. Highway 14 for 1 mile, north on Cedar Avenue for less than a mile, west on 18th Street Southwest for less than a mile to Mosher Avenue and the parking area, on the south side of the road.

Located along the Straight River and Lake Kohlmier, Kaplan's Woods Parkway is a 225-acre park that offers a variety of skiing experiences. The trail system is comprised of a series of interconnected one-way loops that run through open and wooded areas, along the Straight River and its tributary creeks, and around small ponds and wetlands. From the trailhead, the first loop, at the beginner level, is for both skiing and hiking, but after .5 km the hiking trail turns to the east, and the rest of the trails are for skiing only. These are largely suited to the intermediate skier. To the far southeast are two trails for expert skiers.

The Owatonna Parks and Recreation Department also maintains and grooms cross-country ski trails at three other locations: Brooktree Golf Course (3.2 km), Manthey Park (1.6 km), and Mineral Springs Park (1.2 km).

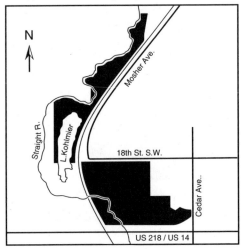

Contact
Owatonna Parks and Recreation Department, 500 Dunnell Drive, Owatonna, MN 55060
(507) 455-0800

42 Keller Regional Park
Maplewood, Minnesota

Trackset: 4.2 km **Skating: 0 km** **Ungroomed: 0 km**

Beginner, Intermediate, Advanced

Location
From I-35E, east on Minnesota Highway 36 for 2 miles, south on U.S. Highway 61 (Maplewood Drive) for .25 mile, east on County Road B for a short distance to the parking lot, on the south side of the road.

The trail system consists of three one-way loops in the golf course. The longer outside loop is suited to the advanced skier, and the two inner loops are at the beginner and intermediate levels of difficulty.

Contact
Ramsey County Parks and Recreation Department, 2015 North Van Dyke Street, Maplewood, MN 55109
(612) 777-1707

Map following page

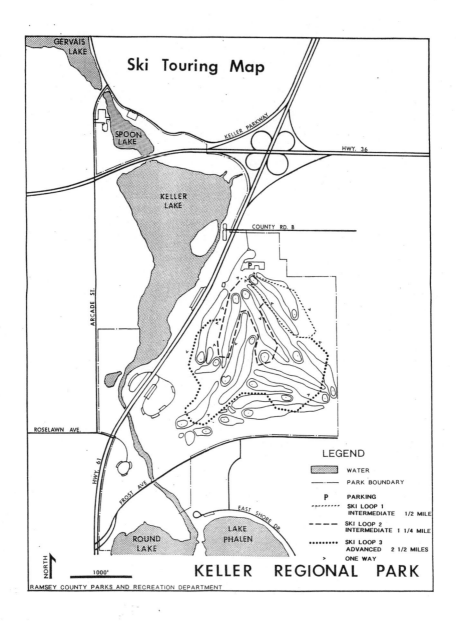

43 Kinnickinnic State Park
River Falls, Wisconsin

Trackset: 0 km   **Skating: 0 km**   **Ungroomed: 10.1 km**

Beginner, Intermediate, Advanced

Location

From St. Paul, east on I-94 to exit 2 for Hudson, south on Carmichael Road for
1.2 miles to the dogtrack, where Carmichael becomes County Road F, continuing
south for 7.5 miles, west on 820th Avenue for .2 mile to the park entrance, on the
south side of the road.

The trail network is composed of one-way loops connected by two-way trails.
Most are very easy, although a couple are at the intermediate level, and one is designed for the advanced skier. The trails run through forests, open land, prairie
restoration areas, and along the banks of the Kinnickinnic and St. Croix rivers.
Many scenic views of forest, beaver ponds, and the river valleys are found
throughout the trails.

Daily or annual Wisconsin State Park permits, required for all vehicles entering a state park, may be purchased at the park office.

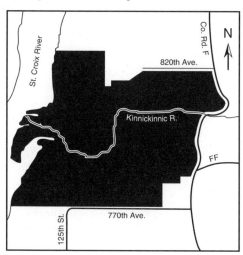

Contact

Kinnickinnic State Park, W. 11983 820th Avenue, River Falls, WI 54022
(715) 425-1129

44 Lake Elmo Park Reserve
Lake Elmo, Minnesota

Trackset: 19 km   **Skating: 5 km**   **Ungroomed: 0 km**

Beginner, Intermediate

Location
In Lake Elmo: from I-94, north on County Road 19 (Keats Avenue) for 1 mile to the park entrance.

The trail system is situated between Lake Elmo and Bald Eagle Lake. Several small lakes and ponds dot the landscape around the trails. The gently rolling terrain offers skiers a variety of experiences and challenges. The reserve combines nature, interpretive, and observation areas, as well as a variety of year-round activities. Like all park reserves, where 80% of the area must be left in a natural state, Lake Elmo Park reserve is actively managed for wildlife. Watch for pheasants, woodpeckers, cardinals, rabbits, squirrels, and deer. There is a shelter with a wood stove and firewood.

Washington County Parks General Information
A parking permit, required for all vehicles entering Washington County parks, may be purchased at the Public Works Department, Lake Elmo Park Reserve, City of Cottage Grove, Forest Lake and Woodbury License Centers, and the Auditor-Treasurer's Office in the Stillwater Government Center. From June through August, permits are available at Square Lake Park and Cottage Grove Ravine Regional Park. Washington County permits are honored in Anoka, Carver, and Hennepin Parks.

    The parks have a few simple rules:
- Skiing hours are from 7:00 a.m. to 30 minutes after sunset.
- Snowmobiling, hiking, sledding, and snowshoeing are not allowed.
- Dogs are not permitted on the ski trails.
- Place litter in the park's waste containers.
- Set fires only in the fire rings or fireplaces.
- Obey the speed limits and park only in designated areas.
- Alcoholic beverages are not permitted in the parks.
- Follow one-way trails in the proper direction.
- Skating is permitted only on designated loops.

Contact
Washington County Parks Section, 1515 Keats Avenue North, Lake Elmo, MN 55042
(612) 731-3851

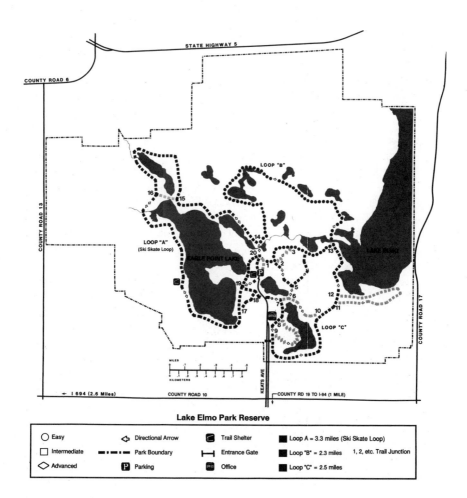

Lake Elmo Park Reserve

○ Easy	◁ Directional Arrow	Trail Shelter	■ Loop A = 3.3 miles (Ski Skate Loop)
□ Intermediate	■ ▪ ■ ▪ Park Boundary	⊢⊣ Entrance Gate	■ Loop "B" = 2.3 miles — 1, 2, etc. Trail Junction
◇ Advanced	P Parking	Office	■ Loop "C" = 2.5 miles

45 Lake Maria State Park
Monticello, Minnesota

Trackset: 20 km   **Skating: 0 km**   **Ungroomed: 0 km**

Beginner, Intermediate

Location

From the Twin Cities, northwest on I-94 for 25 miles to Monticello, east 2 blocks on Minnesota Highway 25, west on County Road 39 for 8 miles, following the signs to the park entrance.

Lake Maria State Park lies within the St. Croix moraine, characterized by a rough, wooded terrain and terminal moraines—accumulations of boulders, stones, sand, and other debris left behind more than 10,000 years ago, when the last glacier retreated—and small lakes, ponds, and marshes in the depressions produced by the glaciers. This habitat is ideal for a variety of wildlife. Lake Maria is in the northern end of what was called the Big Woods, about 3,000 square miles, 100 miles from north to south and 40 miles wide at its southern end. It was very densely forested, covered with maple, basswood, white and red elm, red oak, tamarack in swamps, and red cedar on lake shores. Some of the woods were so dense that sunlight could not penetrate to the forest floor. Today, this land is cleared and farmed. Lake Maria State Park encompasses land that remains today as it was during the early settler period.

The ski trails are laid out in a series of one-way loops, beginning at the parking lot, south of the information center. The loops to the south are for beginners, and those to the north are designed for the intermediate level. A heated trail center provides restrooms and drinking water. Winter camping is permitted at several ski-in sites.

In addition to the ski trails, the park has an ice-skating rink and a sledding hill. With skis, skates, and sleds, a whole day of winter fun can be had at Lake Maria State Park.

Minnesota State Parks General Information

- Parks are open year-round, but the hours vary.
- The use of weapons, traps, or nets is strictly prohibited.
- Pets must be kept on a leash no longer than six feet, and they are not allowed in buildings or on groomed ski trails.
- Motorized vehicles are permitted only on the park roads, not on the trails.
- Do not pick or dig up plants, disturb or feed animals, or scavenge dead wood.
- Daily or annual permits, required for all vehicles entering a state park, may be purchased at the park headquarters or the DNR information center in St. Paul.

Contact

Lake Maria State Park, Route 1, Box 128, Monticello, MN 55362
(612) 878-2325
Department of Natural Resources, Division of Parks and Recreation,
500 Lafayette Road, St. Paul, MN 55155-4040
Metro: 296-6157
Non-metro: (800) 766-6000
TDD metro: 296-5484
TDD non-metro: (800) 657-3929

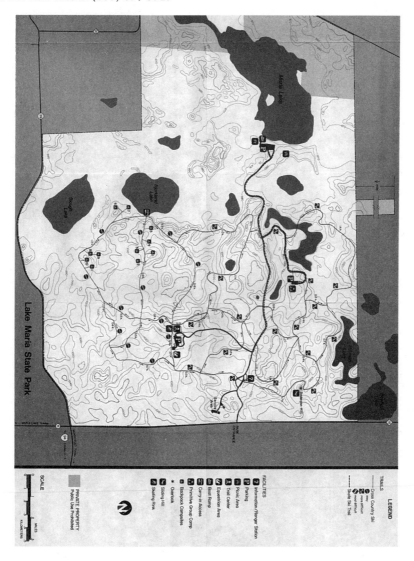

46 Lake Minnewashta Regional Park Chanhassen, Minnesota

Trackset: 9 km   **Skating: 0 km**   **Ungroomed: 0 km**

Beginner, Intermediate

Location
In Chanhassen: From Minnesota Highway 7, south on Minnesota Highway 41 (Hazeltine Boulevard) for 1 mile to the park entrance, on the west side of the road.

Lake Minnewashta Regional Park is still in development. Currently there are nearly 9 km of cross-country ski trails, which run through prairie and marsh, and along Lake Minnewashta.

The shelters and picnic grounds provide water and electric service. One shelter may be reserved for groups. The park is open 8:00 a.m. to 9:00 p.m.

A permit fee is charged for each vehicle entering the park: daily, $3; annual, $14; and senior citizen annual, $7.

Contact
Carver County Parks, 10775 County Road 33, Young America, MN 55397
Metro: (612) 361-1000
Local: (612) 467-3145

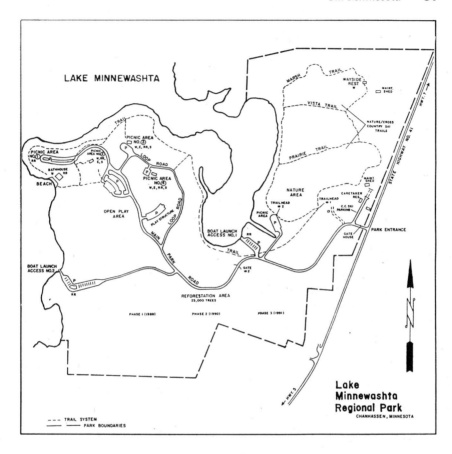

LAKE MINNEWASHTA

Lake
Minnewashta
Regional Park
CHANHASSEN, MINNESOTA

- - - TRAIL SYSTEM
——— PARK BOUNDARIES

47 Lebanon Hills Regional Park Eagan, Minnesota

Trackset: 16.8 km   **Skating: 4 km**   **Ungroomed: 0 km**

Beginner, Intermediate

Location
In Apple Valley and Eagan, with 4 entry points:
- From St. Paul, south on I-35E for 10 miles, east on County Road 32 (Cliff Road) for .5 mile, south on Johnny Cake Ridge Road for .5 mile to the entrance, on the west side of the road.
- From I-35E, east on County Road 32 (Cliff Road) for 2 miles, south on County Road 31 (Pilot Knob Road) for .5 miles to Diamond T Ranch and the entrance, on the east side of the road.
- From I-35E, east on County Road 32 (Cliff Road) for 3 miles to Holland Lake, on the south side of the road.
- From the Holland Lake entrance, east on County Road 32 (Cliff Road) for 1 mile to Schultz Lake, on the south side of the road.

Formerly called Holland-Jensen Park, Lebanon Hills Regional Park encompasses 1,600 acres of land that vary in terrain from gently rolling to quite hilly. Wooded hills, marshlands, and countless small lakes and ponds characterize the park. It is popular with winter birdwatchers. A 1.3 km beginner's loop is located at the Schultz Lake trailhead. More advanced skiers will enjoy the remainder of the trails throughout the West and East Sections of the park. A skating loop of 4 km is located west of Johnny Cake Ridge Road.

Trails are open from 5:00 a.m. to 11:00 p.m. All trailheads have restrooms or toilets, and a warming house with a concession counter is open on weekends at Schultz Lake. Ski equipment can be rented at Diamond T Ranch. Although there are snowmobile and winter hiking trails in the park, they do not interfere with the ski trails.

Dakota County Parks Rules and Regulations
- Ski in the correct, one-way direction.
- Preserve the wildlife.
- Place trash in refuse containers, and recycle all cans.
- Dogs are not permitted on the ski trails.
- Skating is not permitted on tracked trails.
- Fires are permitted only in designated areas.
- Firearms, intoxicating beverages, and all-terrain vehicles are prohibited.

Contact
Dakota County Park Office, 8500 127th Street East, Hastings, MN 55033
(612) 437-6608

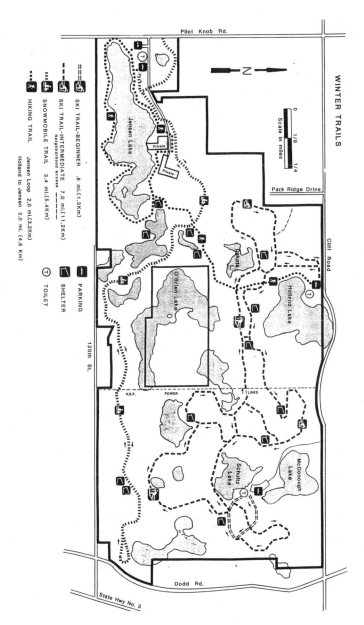

Lebanon Hills Regional Park
(see also next page)

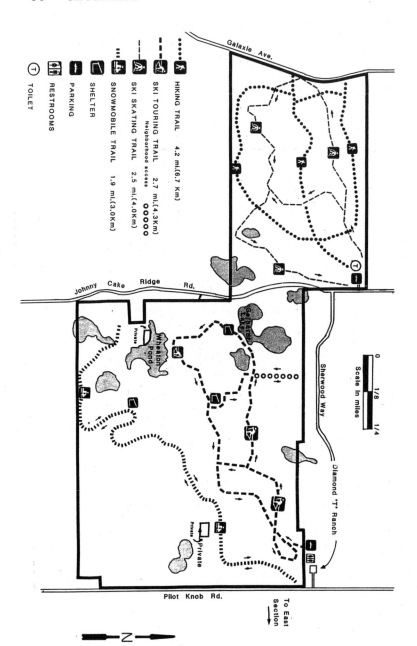

LEBANON HILLS REGIONAL PARK – WEST SECTION

WINTER TRAILS

HIKING TRAIL   4.2 mi.(6.7 Km)

SKI TOURING TRAIL   2.7 mi.(4.3Km)
Neighborhood access   OOOOO

SKI SKATING TRAIL   2.5 mi.(4.0Km)

SNOWMOBILE TRAIL   1.9 mi.(3.0Km)

SHELTER

PARKING

RESTROOMS

TOILET

Scale in miles

0   1/8   1/4

Galaxie Ave.

Johnny   Cake   Ridge   Rd.

Sherwood Way

Diamond "T" Ranch

Pilot   Knob   Rd.

To East
Section

N

48 Lone Lake Park
Minnetonka, Minnesota

Trackset: 4 km   **Skating: 0 km**   **Ungroomed: 0 km**

Intermediate, Advanced

Location
In Minnetonka, from I-494, east on Minnesota Highway 7 for 1 mile, south on County Road 61 (Shady Oak Road) for 1 mile to the park entrance, on the west side of the road.

There are two loops in the system: a loop of 1.3 km for intermediate skiers, and a loop of 2.7 km for advanced skiers. The larger loop is very hilly, and runs along Lone Lake. The only facility offered is a picnic shelter.

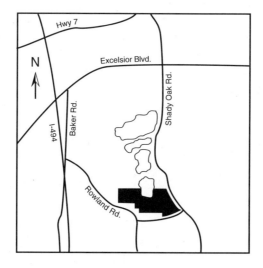

Contact
Minnetonka City Hall, Department of Parks and Recreation, 14600 Minnetonka Boulevard, Minnetonka, MN 55343
(612) 933-2511

49 | Long Lake Regional Park
New Brighton, Minnesota

Trackset: 3.2 km   **Skating: 0 km**   **Ungroomed: 0 km**

Beginner

Location
In New Brighton, from I-694, north on I-35W for 1 mile, west on Minnesota Highway 96 for less than a mile, south on 1st Avenue Northwest for less than a mile, southwest on Old Highway 8 for less than a mile to the park entrance, on the west side of the road.

This beginner-level trail is a series of loops through forest and open land, along marshes and the shores of Rush and Long lakes.

Contact
Ramsey County Parks and Recreation Department, 2015 North Van Dyke Street, Maplewood, MN 55109
(612) 777-1707

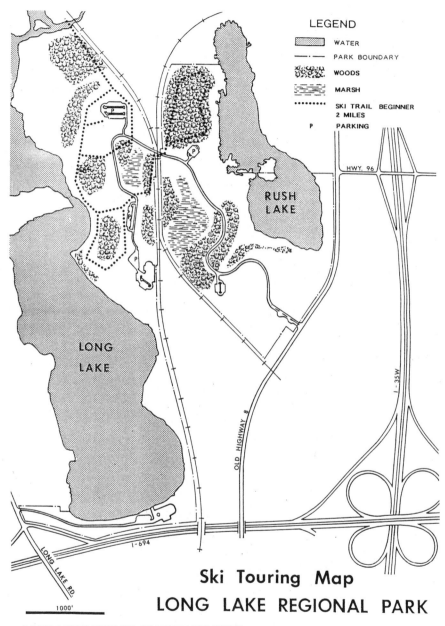

LEGEND

	WATER
	PARK BOUNDARY
	WOODS
	MARSH
	SKI TRAIL BEGINNER 2 MILES
P	PARKING

RUSH LAKE

HWY. 96

LONG LAKE

I - 35W

OLD HIGHWAY 8

I - 694

LONG LAKE RD.

1000'

Ski Touring Map
LONG LAKE REGIONAL PARK

RAMSEY COUNTY PARKS AND RECREATION DEPARTMENT

50 Luce Line State Trail Winsted, Minnesota, to Plymouth, Minnesota

Trackset: 11.5 km   **Skating: 0 km**   **Ungroomed: 0 km**

Beginner

Location
The groomed ski trail runs between Vicksburg Lane in Plymouth and Stubb's Bay Road in Orono, with 2 entry points:
- From I-494, west on U.S. Highway 12 (Wayzata Boulevard) for 2 miles, northeast on County Road 15 (Gleason Lake Road) for 1 mile, north on Vicksburg Lane for 1 mile to the parking lot, on the west side of the road.
- From I-494, west on U.S. Highway 12 (Wayzata Boulevard) for 9 miles, south on Stubbs Bay Road for 1 mile to the parking lot.

In 1902, W. L. Luce began a 1,000-mile trail service for commerce in a large area between Minneapolis and Brookings, South Dakota. In 1913 the Luce Electric Short Line Railway was begun, but because of financial difficulties, the line was terminated in Gluek, a small town northwest of Clara City. Later the line was purchased by the Chicago Northwestern Railroad, but it continued to be financially disastrous and was completely abandoned in 1971.

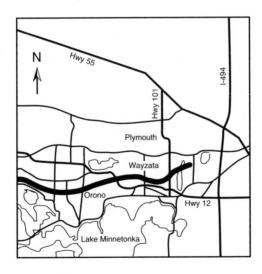

Following the grade of the former railroad, the Luce Line State Trail is a 29-mile-long multi-use recreational trail running between Winsted and Plymouth. It will eventually be extended even further westward. The Luce Line moves through a partly residential area, with a gently rolling terrain dotted by lakes and ponds.

The section of the Luce Line groomed for skiing runs eastward from Stubb's Bay Road. Snowmobiles are allowed on the trail to the west of Stubb's Bay Road.

There are restrooms and picnic areas at the Vicksburg Lane trailhead and at the Wakefield-Conry Rest Area, which is 2 miles east of Stubb's Bay Road.

Contact

Department of Natural Resources, Division of Parks and Recreation,
500 Lafayette Road, St. Paul, MN 55155-4040
Metro: 296-6157
Non-metro: (800) 766-6000
TDD metro: 296-5484
TDD non-metro: (800) 657-3929

51 | Luck Cross Country Ski Trail
Luck, Wisconsin

Trackset: 7.2 km   **Skating: 0 km**   **Ungroomed: 0 km**

Intermediate, Advanced

Location

From Taylors Falls, Minnesota, east on U.S. Highway 8 for 5 miles, north on Wisconsin Highway 35 for 14 miles to Luck, east on Butternut Avenue for less than a mile, south on 7th Street for less than a mile, east on South Shore Drive for less than a mile to the parking lot and clubhouse, on the south side of the road.

The system of trails is laid out in three loops which run through hardwood and pine forests, open land, and around sloughs and ponds. Restrooms and concessions are available at the clubhouse.

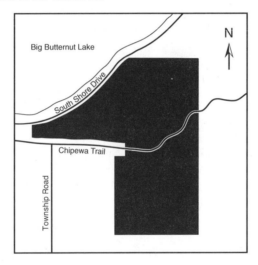

Contact

Luck Recreation Department, Village Hall, 401 Main Street, Luck, WI 54853 (715) 472-2221

52 Manitou Golf Course
White Bear Lake, Minnesota

Trackset: 5.9 km   **Skating: 0 km**   **Ungroomed: 0 km**

Beginner, Intermediate, Advanced

Location
In White Bear Lake, from I-694, north on County Road 65 (White Bear Avenue) for .5 mile, east on Orchard Lane for .5 mile, south on McKnight Road for .5 mile to the parking lot, on the east side of the road.

This trails consists of three one-way loops. The initial loop, of 1 km, is for beginners. The next loop, of 3.2 km, is of intermediate difficulty. The farthest loop, of 1.7 km, will challenge expert skiers. All three loops run along the golf course's fairways and ponds. Restrooms are available at the clubhouse.

Contact
Ramsey County Parks and Recreation Department, 2015 North Van Dyke Street, Maplewood, MN 55109
(612) 777-1707

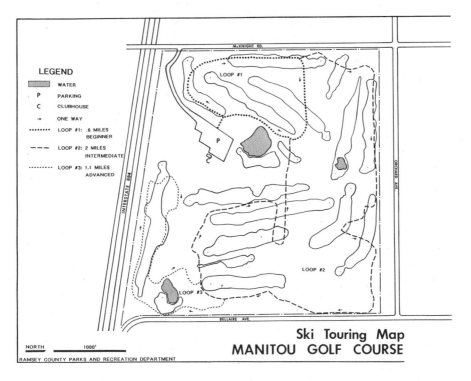

Ski Touring Map
MANITOU GOLF COURSE

53 Marsh Lake Park Trail System
Bloomington, Minnesota

Trackset: 0 km   **Skating: 0 km**   **Ungroomed: 1.1 km**

Beginner

Location

From I-494, south on County Road 17 (France Avenue) for 1.5 miles, east on West 98th Street for less than a mile to the park entrance, on the north side of the road.

These trails run throughout the park's lowlands and ponds. Although they are not groomed, their gentle terrain makes them suitable for beginners.

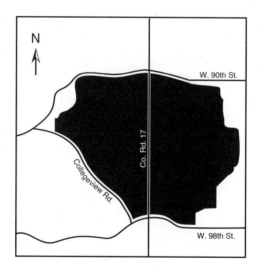

Contact

City of Bloomington, Parks and Recreation Division, 2215 West Old Shakopee Road, Bloomington, MN 55431
(612) 887-9638

54 Meadow Park
Minnetonka, Minnesota

Trackset: 2.9 km **Skating: 0 km** **Ungroomed: 0 km**

Beginner

Location
In Minnetonka, from I-494, east on County Road 5 (Minnetonka Boulevard) for less than a mile, north on Oakland Road for less than a mile to Stone Road and the parking lot, on the east side of the road.

The trail is a single one-way loop through flat, wooded marshland. There is a warming house at the park.

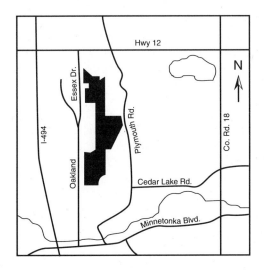

Contact
Minnetonka City Hall, Department of Parks and Recreation, 14600 Minnetonka Boulevard, Minnetonka, MN 55343
(612) 933-2511

55 | Mineral Springs Park
Owatonna, Minnesota

Trackset: 1.2 km   **Skating: 0 km**   **Ungroomed: 0 km**

Beginner

Location
In Owatonna, northeast on Cherry Street to the park entrance.

Mineral Springs Park, the most well-known of the Owatonna parks, came into being both as a resort area and a business venture. In 1875 the Owatonna Mineral Springs Company was organized. This company secured the services of an expert chemist who analyzed the spring waters and pronounced them very similar to the waters of the famed Vichy Springs in the Ardennes of France. The Owatonna water was served for many years in dining cars of the railroads.

A special feature of the park is the "car wash," which is a hard-surfaced area built in the stream bed of Maple Creek for the sole purpose of washing vehicles. In the 1970s an artificial waterfall was constructed, a gift from Reuben A. Kaplan.

The trail system encompasses a stretch of Maple Creek, a tributary of the Straight River. The park has restrooms and two picnic shelters, one with grills and electricity.

The Owatonna Parks and Recreation Department maintains and grooms cross-country ski trails at three other locations: Brooktree Golf Course (3.2 km), Kaplan's Woods Parkway (13.5 km), and Manthey Park (1.6 km).

Contact
Owatonna Parks and Recreation Department, 500 Dunnell Drive, Owatonna, MN 55060
(507) 455-0800

56 Minnesota Landscape Arboretum Chanhassen, Minnesota

Trackset: 10 km **Skating: 0 km** **Ungroomed: 0 km**

Beginner, Intermediate, Advanced

Location
From I-494, west on Minnesota Highway 5 for 9 miles to the entrance, on the south side of the road.

The trails of the Minnesota Landscape Arboretum meander through rolling hills in 900 acres of forest, prairie, marsh, and open land and around bogs and ponds. The extensive Minnesota plant collection is unique among ski trails in the area. The arboretum is a research facility, so the plants must not be disturbed. The trail of even one skier can damage some of the plants.

All trails begin at the Snyder Building, which is open from 8:00 a.m. to 4:30 p.m. on weekdays and 11:00 a.m. to 4:30 p.m. on weekends. Trail maps are available at the front desk: there are few signs on the trails. The Tearoom, which serves light lunches and desserts, is open from 11:30 a.m. to 1:30 p.m. daily.

Contact
Minnesota Landscape Arboretum, 3675 Arboretum Drive, Chanhassen, MN 55317
(612) 443-2460

Map following page

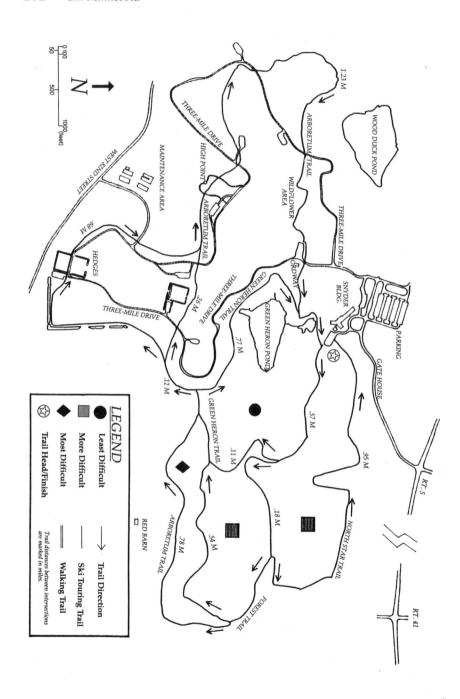

57 | Minnesota Valley Trail State Park
Jordan, Minnesota

Trackset: 0 km   **Skating: 0 km**   **Ungroomed: 14.4 km**

Beginner, Intermediate

The Minnesota River valley was shaped by Glacial River Warren nearly 10,000 years ago, producing a bottomland over 5 miles wide and 300 feet deep in places. The valley contains floodplain marshes, wet meadows, and lakes, and the hills and bluffs support prairies and woodlands, and provide countless vistas for the visitor. The variety of lush vegetation offers a rich wildlife habitat for feeding, breeding, nesting, growth, and wintering of many types of animal life.

The Minnesota Valley Trail, begun in 1969, "provides access to or passage through areas which have significant scenic, historic, scientific, or recreational qualities." The completed trail will follow the Minnesota River Valley for nearly 75 miles, from Fort Snelling State Park to the city of LeSueur. At present, skiing is permitted only at the adjoining Louisville Swamp–Carver Rapids and Lawrence State Waysides in Scott County. Snowmobiles are allowed on separate trails. These snowmobile trails are often used as skating trails because of the well-packed snow, increasing the length of ski trails to 50 km.

Louisville Swamp–Carver Rapids
State Wayside

Location

From Shakopee, south on U.S. Highway 169 for 9 miles to the entrance, on the west side of the road.

The trail system is located on the bluff, and Sand Creek passes through the area on its way to the Minnesota River. There are two loops for skiing only. One of them encircles the Louisville Swamp Unit of the Minnesota Valley National Wildlife Refuge and terminates at the Jabs Farm Homestead Historic Site. The trailhead provides a shelter and restrooms.

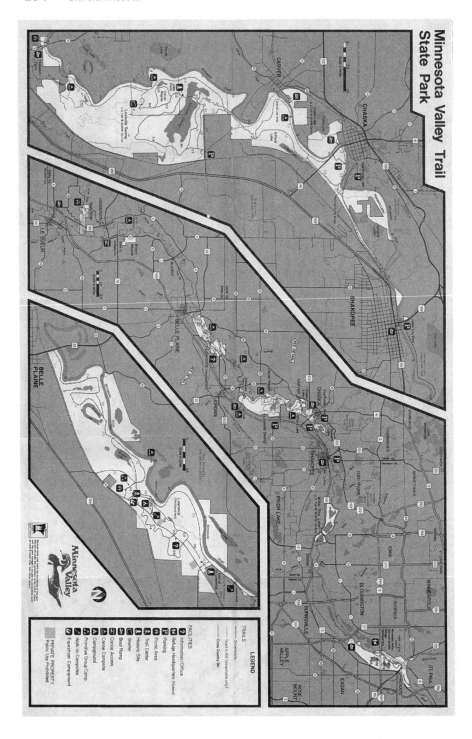

Lawrence State Wayside

Location
From Jordan, north on County Road 9 for .5 mile, west on County Road 57 for 3 miles to the trailhead, on the west side of the road.

Lawrence State Wayside is on a flat floodplain of deciduous trees interspersed with meadows. From trail center, southwest of the wayside office, the ski trails wind through the woods and pass by small marshy ponds. The farthest spur of the trail ends at the Town of St. Lawrence Historic Site.

Minnesota State Parks General Information
• The parks are open year-round, but the hours vary.
• The use of weapons, traps, or nets is strictly prohibited.
• Pets must be kept on a leash no longer than six feet, and they are not allowed in the buildings or on the groomed ski trails.
• Motorized vehicles are permitted only on the park roads, not on the trails.
• Do not pick or dig up plants, disturb or feed animals, or scavenge dead wood.
• Daily or annual permits, required for all vehicles entering a state park, may be purchased at the park headquarters or the information center in St. Paul.

Contact
Minnesota Valley Trail Manager, 19825 Park Boulevard, Jordan, MN 55352
(612) 492-6400
Department of Natural Resources, Division of Parks and Recreation,
500 Lafayette Road, St. Paul, MN 55155-4040
Metro: 296-6157
Non-metro: (800) 766-6000
TDD metro: 296-5484
TDD non-metro: (800) 657-3929

58 | Minnesota Zoological Garden Apple Valley, Minnesota

Trackset: 10 km   **Skating: 2 km**   **Ungroomed: 0 km**

Beginner, Intermediate, Advanced

Location
From Minneapolis, south on Minnesota Highway 77 (Cedar Avenue) past I-35E, following signs to the zoo.

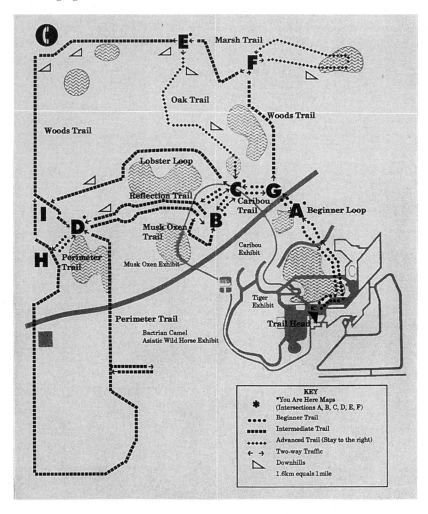

Marsh Trail
Oak Trail
Woods Trail
Woods Trail
Lobster Loop
Reflection Trail
Caribou Trail
Beginner Loop
Musk Oxen Trail
Caribou Exhibit
Perimeter Trail
Musk Oxen Exhibit
Tiger Exhibit
Perimeter Trail
Trail Head
Bactrian Camel
Asiatic Wild Horse Exhibit

KEY
✳ *You Are Here Maps (Intersections A, B, C, D, E, F)
•••• Beginner Trail
▪▪▪▪▪ Intermediate Trail
♦♦♦♦♦ Advanced Trail (Stay to the right)
← → Two-way Traffic
◁ Downhills
1.6km equals 1 mile

The Minnesota Zoo's trails are well marked and groomed. They surely must be the state's most unusual system: you can see moose, Bactrian camels, musk oxen, snow monkeys, caribou, Siberian tigers, Asiatic wild horses, and red pandas near the trails. The terrain is varied and involves beautiful hilly woodland, marshes, and gently rolling meadows. The beginners trails are short and easy. The system is mainly intermediate in difficulty, but there are two long, exciting trails with steep hills for advanced skiers.

Besides the excitement on the trails, there are many indoor zoo exhibits. The main building also has food, snacks, and restrooms.

There is an admission fee for the zoo and its ski trails: no charge for ages 2 and younger, $2.50 for ages 3-12, $6 for ages 13-64, and $4 for ages 65 and older. Ski equipment for the entire family may be rented at $3.50 per hour with a 2-hour minimum, with no skis rented after 3:00 p.m. Lessons are also available. The zoo is open for skiing daily from 9:00 a.m. to 3:00 p.m., except on Christmas Day or in bad weather. Skiers may stay on the trails past 3:00 p.m., but no new skiers may enter the zoo thereafter. Snowshoes and sleds are not permitted on the ski trails.

Contact

Minnesota Zoological Garden, 13000 Zoo Boulevard, Apple Valley,
MN 55124-8199
Administrative Offices: (612) 431-9200
Zoo-To-Do Hotline: (612) 432-9000

59 Montissippi County Park
Monticello, Minnesota

Trackset: 2.3 km   **Skating: 0 km**   **Ungroomed: 0 km**

Beginner

Location

From Minneapolis: northwest on I-94 for 22 miles to Monticello, northwest on County Road 75 for 2 miles to the park entrance, on the east side of the road.

Set along the Mississippi River, Montissippi County Park is 170 acres of hardwood forest and pine tree plantings. The two loops of ski trails pass through the pines and along the river.

The park facilities include a picnic area and restrooms.

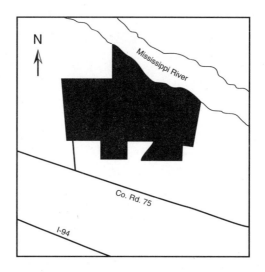

Contact

Wright County Parks Department, 3554 Braddock Avenue Northeast, Buffalo, MN 55313
Local: (612) 682-7693
Metro: 339-6881
Toll-free: (800) 362-3667

60 Mound Springs Park Trail System
Bloomington, Minnesota

Trackset: 0 km   **Skating: 0 km**   **Ungroomed: 5.3 km**

Beginner, Intermediate, Advanced

Location

Five entry points, with parking along the street:

• At 11th Avenue South and East 100th Street, on the east side of the intersection.

• At 10th Avenue Circle and 102nd Street, on the southeast side of the intersection.

• Near Columbus Road and Park Avenue South, on the southeast side of the intersection.

• At Hopkins Road and Hopkins Circle, on the southwest side of the intersection.

• At the terminus of Lyndale Avenue South, the junction of the Mound Springs Park Trail and the Central Park–Nine Mile Creek Trail, on the east side of the road.

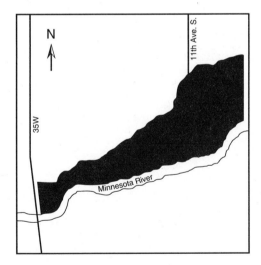

The park, located on a steep headland overlooking the Minnesota River Valley, is the site of Native American burial mounds from a very early time. The mound area should be treated with respect.

From the main trailhead, the first .5 mile descends to the Minnesota River bottom, and is very steep and narrow, with switchbacks. All skiers, even those with advanced skills, must use extreme caution on this stretch, and most skiers should remove theirs skis and walk to the bottom. The terrain at the river bottom is fairly flat with some gentle undulation. The trail is well marked but not groomed. The trail passes through a deciduous forest of primarily upland hardwoods. At the river bottom, the trees are mainly elm and basswood.

Limited parking is available on streets at the trail access points. There are no toilets or water at the trailhead.

Contact
City of Bloomington, Parks and Recreation Division, 2215 West Old Shakopee Road, Bloomington, MN 55431
(612) 887-9638

61 Mount Normandale Lake Park Bloomington, Minnesota

Trackset: 0 km   **Skating: 0 km**   **Ungroomed: 5.3 km**

Beginner

Location
At the northern end of Hyland Lake Park Reserve, with two entry points:
- On West 84th Street, between Normandale Boulevard and East Bush Lake Road.
- On Chalet Road, one block south of the intersection of West 84th Street and East Bush Lake Road.

The trail, a loop around Mount Normandale Lake, is flat, with one or two very gradual inclines. It moves woods and lakeshore meadows crossed by Nine Mile Creek. The trail serves as a bike path during the warmer seasons. Although it is not groomed, it is well marked. The park has no water or restrooms.

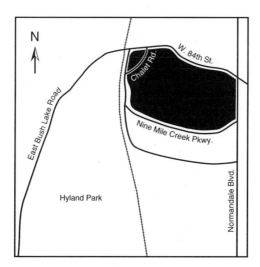

Contact
City of Bloomington, Parks and Recreation Division, 2215 West Old Shakopee Road, Bloomington, MN 55431 (612) 887-9638

62 Murphy-Hanrehan Park Reserve Savage, Minnesota

Trackset: 20 km   **Skating: 20 km**   **Ungroomed: 0 km**

Intermediate, Advanced

Location

From Burnsville, west on County Road 42 for 3 miles from I-35W, south on County Road 74 (Hanrehan Lake Boulevard) for 3 miles, southeast on County Road 75 for 1 mile to the trailhead, on the east side of the road.

Murphy-Hanrehan has earned respect in the skiing community as one of the most challenging and exhilarating trail systems in Minnesota. The innermost loops are well suited to skiers of intermediate skill, but most of the trails, especially the outside loop, provide a good workout for even the most advanced skiers. Designed for serious conditioning and training, the steep uphill grades and downhill runs will test skiers' skills. Nearly all downhill runs are extremely steep, and many have curves at the bottom or proceed up another hill immediately. For the sake of safety, skiers must follow all directional signs scrupulously. When trail conditions deteriorate, the staff closes certain trails by shutting gates at their entrances and exits. Skiers must not venture beyond these closed gates, for even the slightest change in conditions may make trails very hazardous. The landscape is heavily wooded with oak and other hardwoods, and includes numerous small ponds nestled in depressions.

A heated trail center at the trailhead has maps, restrooms, and a snack bar. It is open from 2:00 p.m. to 5:00 p.m. on weekdays and from 9:00 a.m. to 5:00 p.m. on weekends.

Hennepin County Parks General Information

Trails are open from 8:00 a.m. to sunset. Some parks designate certain nights for moonlight or lantern skiing. All trails and accesses are open on holidays; however, trailheads, visitor centers, and other facilities close early or do not open on Thanksgiving Day, Christmas Eve, and Christmas Day.

Many of the parks offer a full progression of ski lessons for children and adults, including instruction in classic and skating. To rent skis, boots, and poles, a picture ID is required. In addition to on-the-trail lessons, several indoor programs teach a variety of skiing basics, including an introduction to cross-country skiing, ski skating, telemark skiing, and ski waxing. There are also many non-skiing programs, such as snowshoeing and deer watching, for children and adults.

A parking fee is charged at all parks: daily, $4; annual, $20; senior citizens annual, $13. The first Tuesday of each month is a free day in all parks: no parking

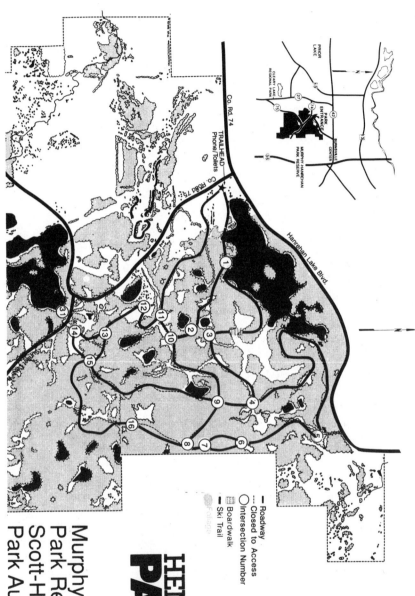

Murphy-Hanrehan
Park Reserve
Scott-Hennepin
Park Authority

HENNEPIN
PARKS

fees are charged. When a holiday falls on the first Tuesday of a month, the second Tuesday is a free day. Hennepin Parks permits are honored at Washington, Anoka, and Carver county parks. Washington and Anoka county parks permits are valid at Hennepin Parks facilities. When displayed with a $4 "Star" permit, Carver County permits are valid at Hennepin Parks.

The parks have a few simple rules:
• Ski during park operating hours only.
• Ski only on groomed trails and follow all directional signs.
• Dogs are not permitted on the ski trails.
• Ski trails are designed and maintained for skiing only. Hiking, sledding, snow-shoeing, and snowmobiling can ruin a good ski track.

Contact
Hennepin Parks, 18106 Texas Avenue, Prior Lake, MN 55372 (612) 447-6913
Hennepin Parks Administration Office, general information for all parks: (612) 559-9000
Reservations for lessons and programs: (612) 559-6700
TDD: (612) 559-6719
Trail conditions hotline for all parks: (612) 559-6778

63 Nerstrand Big Woods State Park Nerstrand, Minnesota

Trackset: 13 km   Skating: 0 km   Ungroomed: 0 km

Beginner, Intermediate

Location
From Northfield, southeast on Minnesota Highway 246 for 12 miles, following the signs to the park entrance, on the west side of the road.

The park takes its name from the nearby small town of Nerstrand. The town was founded in 1855 by a Norwegian immigrant named Osmund Osmundson. He chose to call the village Nerstrand after his former seaport home in Norway. Deep nostalgia and loyalty were more important than the name's propriety; it means "near the sea."

Most of the park is heavily forested with nearly every tree species native to Minnesota, though hardwoods dominate. This is one of the last remnants of the Big Woods that once covered south central Minnesota. Its hilly terrain is part of a system of glacial moraines. The Prairie Creek threads through the park and has cut a scenic valley that offers many picturesque views, some with waterfalls.

The ski trails are north of the park's main road. At the picnic ground a fairly short loop proceeds across Hickory Bridge, where there is a waterfall. Four loops on the other side of the bridge comprise Fawn Trail and Beaver Trail. In warmer seasons Easy Walker Trail accommodates wheelchairs and strollers. Snowmobiling is permitted on separate trails in the southern half of the park; they do not intermingle with the ski trails.

Minnesota State Parks General Information
- The parks are open year-round, but the hours vary.
- The use of weapons, traps, or nets is strictly prohibited.
- Pets must be kept on a leash no longer than six feet, and they are not allowed in the buildings or on the groomed ski trails.
- Motorized vehicles are permitted only on the park roads, not on the trails.
- Do not pick or dig up plants, disturb or feed animals, or scavenge dead wood.
- Daily or annual permits, required for all vehicles entering a state park, may be purchased at the park headquarters or the information center in St. Paul.

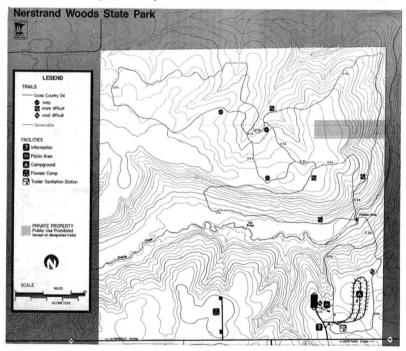

Contact
Nerstrand Woods State Park, 9700 170th Street East, Nerstrand, MN 55053 (507) 334-8848

Department of Natural Resources, Division of Parks and Recreation, 500 Lafayette Road, St. Paul, MN 55155-4040

Metro: 296-6157   TDD metro: 296-5484

Non-metro: (800) 766-6000   TDD non-metro: (800) 657-3929

64 | Nugget Lake County Park
Plum City, Wisconsin

Trackset: 11.2 km   **Skating: 0 km**   **Ungroomed: 0 km**

Beginner, Intermediate, Advanced

Location
From St. Paul, east on I-94 for 31 miles, south on U.S. Highway 63 for 16 miles, east on Wisconsin Highway 72 for 11 miles, south on County Road S for 3 miles, west on County Road HH for 1 mile to the park entrance, on the south side of the road.

Neighboring Nugget Lake was the result of the 1972 construction of a large flood control dam. It was named in honor of the gold mining of the late 1800s.

The terrain of this well-forested, 750-acre park varies from flat to gently rolling to very hilly. The trails run in a series of loops along Rock Elm Creek and Plum Creek, passing several scenic overlooks of Nugget Lake and Blue Rock geological formations, a beaver dam, and a deer feeding area; they range from steep, winding trails to flat, gentle terrain. Benches are scattered throughout the trail network. Restrooms are available at the trailhead. Winter camping is permitted.

Daily or annual park permits, required for all vehicles entering the park, may be purchased at the park office.

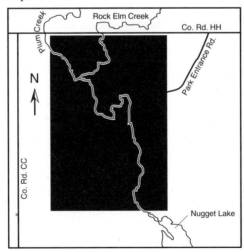

Contact
Nugget Lake County Park, N4351 County Road HH, Plum City, WI 54761
(715) 639-5611

65 Oakdale Park
Oakdale, Minnesota

Trackset: 7.2 km   **Skating: 0 km**   **Ungroomed: 0 km**

Beginner, Intermediate, Advanced

Location
From St. Paul on I-694, west on Minnesota Highway 36 for 1 mile, south on Division Avenue for .5 mile, east on 45th Street for .5 mile to the park entrance.

The trails are laid out in many one-way loops, through marshy areas and along the shores of a lake. The park is in a residential neighborhood, so skiers are never far from facilities of all kinds.

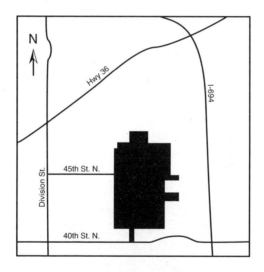

Contact
City of Oakdale, 1584 Hadley Avenue North, Oakdale, MN 55128
(612) 730-2700

66 Phalen Regional Park
St. Paul, Minnesota

Trackset: 10 km   **Skating: 6 km**   **Ungroomed: 0 km**

Beginner, Intermediate

Location
From I-35E, east on Wheelock Parkway for 1.5 miles, north on Phalen Drive for less than a mile to the chalet, on the west side of the road.

All trails are in the golf course. The majority of the trails are of intermediate level, but a few beginner tracks are open just north of the chalet on Sunday through Friday and Saturday after 1:30 p.m. Phalen is also the site of races and several racing clinics.

The chalet, a warm retreat with rental equipment, concessions, and restrooms, offers beginner, intermediate, and skating lessons, individually or in groups, with or without equipment. The chalet is open from 9:00 a.m. to 6:00 p.m. on Saturday, from 11:00 a.m. to 6:00 p.m. on Sunday, and from 5:00 p.m. to 9:00 p.m. on Tuesday.

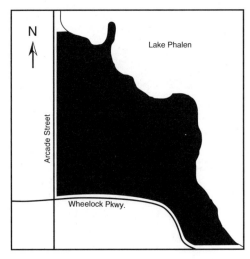

Contact
Phalen Golf Course, 1615 Phalen Drive, Saint Paul, MN 55106
(612) 778-0424
City of Saint Paul, Division of Parks and Recreation, 25 West 4th Street, Room 200, St. Paul, MN 55102
(612) 292-7445

67 Pine Point Park
Stillwater, Minnesota

Trackset: 8 km   **Skating: 0 km**   **Ungroomed: 0 km**

Beginner, Intermediate, Advanced

Location

From Stillwater, north on County Road 55 (Norell Avenue North) for 5 miles to the park's entrance, on the west side of the road.

Most of the trails in Pine Point Park are at the beginner or intermediate level, but one trail, which cuts through the middle of the system, is advanced. The trails move through heavily wooded areas between Loon and Louise lakes and skirt portions of the shores. Some of the land is open meadow framed by the woods, and in other places the canopy of pine trees creates a tunnel-like effect. The hills are gentle to fairly challenging. At the trailhead are maps, picnic tables, barbecue grills, and toilets.

Washington County Parks General Information

A parking permit, required for all vehicles entering Washington County parks, may be purchased at the Public Works Department, Lake Elmo Park Reserve, City of Cottage Grove, Forest Lake and Woodbury License Centers, and the Auditor-Treasurer's Office in the Stillwater Government Center. From June through August, permits are available at Square Lake Park and Cottage Grove Ravine Regional Park. Washington County permits are honored in Anoka, Carver, and Hennepin Parks.

   The parks have a few simple rules:
• Skiing hours are from 7:00 a.m. to 30 minutes after sunset.
• Snowmobiling, hiking, sledding, and snowshoeing are not allowed.
• Dogs are not permitted on the ski trails.
• Place litter in the park's waste containers.
• Set fires only in the fire rings or fireplaces.
• Obey the speed limits and park only in designated areas.
• Alcoholic beverages are not permitted in the parks.
• Follow one-way trails in the proper direction.
• Skating is permitted only on designated loops.

Contact

Washington County Parks Section, 1515 Keats Avenue North, Lake Elmo, MN 55042
(612) 731-3851

Map following page

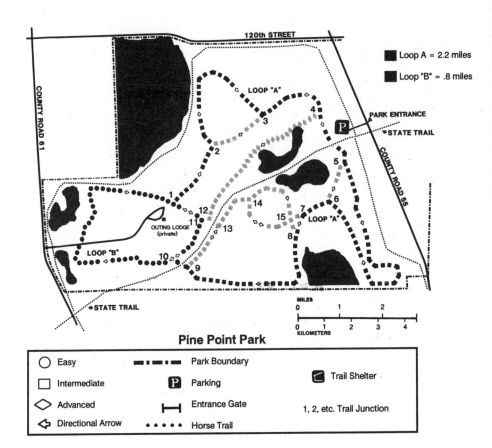

Pine Point Park

○ Easy	▬ ▬ ▬ Park Boundary	◩ Trail Shelter
☐ Intermediate	🅿 Parking	
◇ Advanced	⊢ Entrance Gate	1, 2, etc. Trail Junction
◁ Directional Arrow	• • • • Horse Trail	

68 Pine Tree Apple Orchard
Dellwood, Minnesota

Trackset: 12 km   **Skating: 12 km**   **Ungroomed: 0 km**

Intermediate

Location
From I-694, north on Minnesota Highway 61 for 4 miles, east on Minnesota Highway 96 for 1.5 miles, north on Apple Orchard Road for 1.5 miles to the parking lot, on the east side of the road.

The trail loops pass through apple trees, pine trees, a strawberry patch, and a pumpkin patch, on rolling hills overlooking the north shore of Pine Tree Lake.
   The warming house offers restrooms, hot cider, and an apple pie bakery.

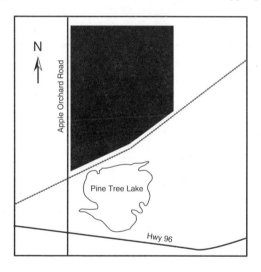

Contact
Pine Tree Apple Orchard, 450 Apple Orchard Road, White Bear Lake, MN 55110
(612) 429-6577

69 Purgatory Creek Park
Minnetonka, Minnesota

Trackset: 2.8 km   **Skating: 0 km**   **Ungroomed: 0 km**

Beginner, Intermediate, Advanced

Location
In Minnetonka, from Minnesota Highway 7, south on Minnesota Highway 101 for .2 mile, east on County Road 3 (Excelsior Boulevard) for .2 mile to the trailhead, on the south side of the road.

From the trailhead a large novice loop crosses a small bridge almost immediately. At the far end of the loop, where the beginner loop continues around to the north, an intermediate loop veers off to the right. The intermediate loop leads to the advanced trails, at the southern end of the park. The three loops are all one-way.

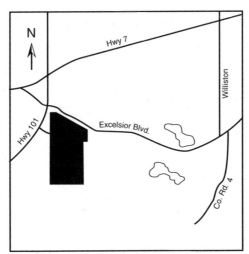

Contact
Minnetonka City Hall, Department of Parks and Recreation, 14600 Minnetonka Boulevard, Minnetonka, MN 55343
(612) 933-2511

70 Rice Lake State Park
Owatonna, Minnesota

Trackset: 5.6 km   **Skating: 0 km**   **Ungroomed: 0 km**

Beginner

Location
From Owatonna, east on County Road 19 for 7 miles to the park entrance, on the south side of the road.

Rice Lake, very shallow with marshy shores, is perfect for migratory waterfowl for resting and feeding. It is also the only lake of its kind for many miles that these birds can use as a stopping point during migrations, so many birds can be seen here in the spring and autumn. During the winter, skiers may glimpse some of the park's many deer.

The marked and groomed trails, three connected loops, move along the shores of Rice Lake, and through deciduous forest and meadows. They involve the picnic grounds, the campgrounds, and the beach and boat landing. The snowmobiling trails are separate and intersect the ski trails at only two points.

Minnesota State Parks General Information
- The parks are open year-round, but the hours vary.
- The use of weapons, traps, or nets is strictly prohibited.
- Pets must be kept on a leash no longer than six feet, and they are not allowed in the buildings or on the groomed ski trails.
- Motorized vehicles are permitted only on the park roads, not on the trails.
- Do not pick or dig up plants, disturb or feed animals, or scavenge dead wood.
- Daily or annual permits, required for all vehicles entering a state park, may be purchased at the park headquarters or the information center in St. Paul.

Contact
Rice Lake State Park, Route 3, Owatonna, MN 55060
(507) 451-7406
Department of Natural Resources, Division of Parks and Recreation,
500 Lafayette Road, St. Paul, MN 55155-4040
Metro: 296-6157
Non-metro: (800) 766-6000
TDD metro: 296-5484
TDD non-metro: (800) 657-3929

Map following page

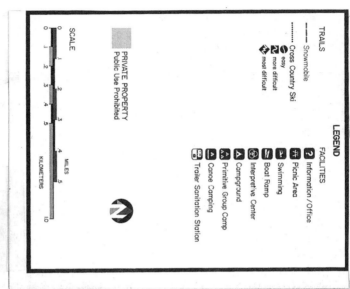

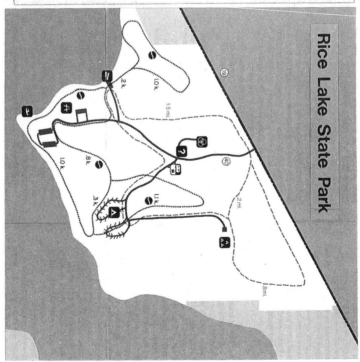

71 Ritter Farm Park
Lakeville, Minnesota

Trackset: 12 km **Skating: 6 km** **Ungroomed: 0 km**

Beginner, Intermediate, Advanced

Location
From Minneapolis, south on I-35 for 15 miles to the Lakeville exit (185th Street), west and south on the frontage road for .5 mile to 195th Street and the park access road, on the north side of the road.

The trails, designed by international ski trail advisors, offer challenges to skiers of all abilities. They are well marked and are groomed several times a week by the Lakeville Park Department. Ritter Farm was once crop and grazing lands, as indicated by some old woodlots, groves, and orchards. The terrain varies from flat to gently rolling to extremely hilly, with thick woods and open meadows. The heated trail center has restrooms.

A parking fee is charged for each vehicle entering the park, and annual permits may be purchased.

A snowmobile trail crosses ski trails at three points. For the most part, however, it runs along the border of the park, far from the ski trails.

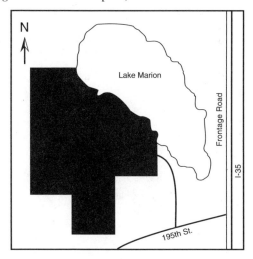

Contact
Lakeville Parks and Recreation Department, 8747 208th Street, Lakeville, MN 55044
(612) 469-4431

72 River Bend Nature Center Faribault, Minnesota

Trackset: 16 km**Skating: 0 km****Ungroomed: 0 km**

Beginner, Intermediate, Advanced

Location

In Faribault, from I-35, east on Minnesota Highway 60 for 1 mile to downtown Faribault, continue east on Minnesota Highway 60 across the Straight River, east on Division Street for less than a mile, south on 10th Avenue Southeast for less than a mile, east on 5th Street Southeast for less than a mile, south and east on Rustad Road for 1 mile to the entrance.

River Bend Nature Center is a fine example of cooperation between private citizens and city government. A Bicentennial project for the city of Faribault, this 650-acre preserve is comprised of prairie, wetlands, and woodlands of maple, basswood, cottonwood, elm, and willow. The valley of the Straight River is also featured in the nature center.

The well-marked ski trails are situated on a terrain that is varied but fairly level on the average. Many of them run along the banks of the Straight River.

The main building has restrooms and maps.

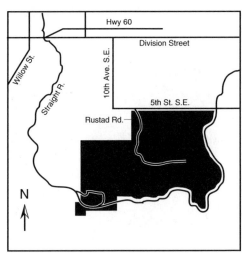

Contact

River Bend Nature Center, Box 265, Faribault, MN 55021
(507) 332-7151

73 Robert Ney Memorial Park Reserve Maple Lake, Minnesota

Trackset: 4.8 km   **Skating: 0 km**   **Ungroomed: 0 km**

Beginner

Location

From Minneapolis, northwest on Minnesota Highway 55 for 30 miles to Maple Lake, north on County Road 8 for 4 miles to the park entrance, on the east side of the road.

Occupying 320 acres of land along the shore of Lake Mary, Robert Ney Memorial Park Reserve offers a variety of terrain, vegetation, and wildlife. The ski trail network is laid out in a series of loops that move through a hardwood forest and some pine tree plantings, and along the banks of Silver Creek. They are all designed for beginners. The park has a picnic area, but no heated shelter or restrooms.

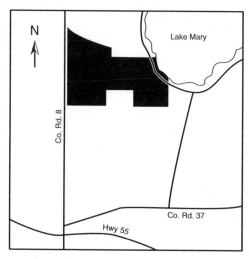

Contact

Wright County Parks Department, 3554 Braddock Avenue Northeast, Buffalo, MN 55313
Local: (612) 682-7693
Metro: 339-6881
Toll-free: (800) 362-3667

74 Sakatah Lake State Park
Waterville, Minnesota

Trackset: 11 km   **Skating: 0 km**   **Ungroomed: 0 km**

Beginner, Intermediate, Advanced

Location
From I-35, west on Minnesota Highway 60 from Faribault for 14 miles to the park entrance, on the north side of the road.

Sakatah Lake State Park preserves a remnant of the Big Woods that once covered east central Minnesota and the Mississippi River Valley. The park, a hilly region of glacial moraines, offers the opportunity to see Minnesota as it looked to the first white settlers. The forest species of hardwoods such as oak, maple, basswood, and walnut is like an enormous canopy around the Sakatah Lakes. These lakes are natural widenings of the Cannon River. The park is near the setting of Laura Ingalls Wilder's first book, *Little House in the Big Woods*.

The trails, used for hiking in warmer months, are easy to follow. They are set up in two sections, and skirt the lakeshore of Upper Sakatah Lake and circle the campground. The system involves many hills and the heavy woodlands of the region. The Sakatah Singing Hills State Trail runs along the northern edge of the park, crossing the ski trails twice.

Minnesota State Parks General Information
- The parks are open year-round, but the hours vary.
- The use of weapons, traps, or nets is strictly prohibited.
- Pets must be kept on a leash no longer than six feet, and they are not allowed in the buildings or on the groomed ski trails.
- Motorized vehicles are permitted only on the park roads, not on the trails.
- Do not pick or dig up plants, disturb or feed animals, or scavenge dead wood.
- Daily or annual permits, required for all vehicles entering a state park, may be purchased at the park headquarters or the information center in St. Paul.

Contact
Sakatah Lake State Park, Route 2, Box 19, Waterville, MN 56096
(507) 362-4438
Department of Natural Resources, Division of Parks and Recreation,
500 Lafayette Road, St. Paul, MN 55155-4040
Metro: 296-6157   TDD metro: 296-5484
Non-metro: (800) 766-6000   TDD non-metro: (800) 657-3929

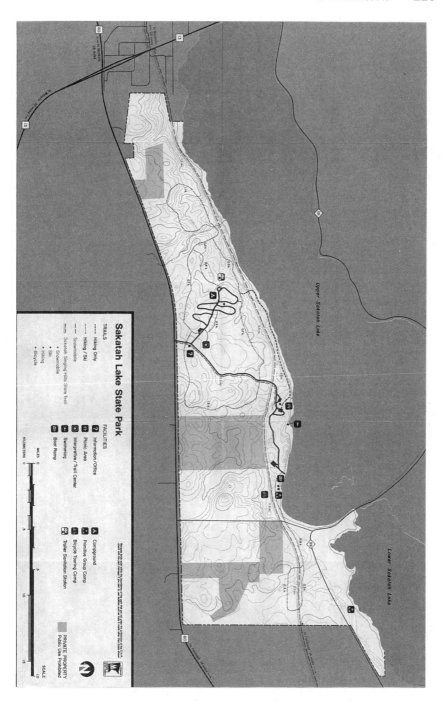

75 Sakatah Singing Hills State Trail Mankato, Minnesota to Faribault, Minnesota

Trackset: 0 km   **Skating: 0 km**   **Ungroomed: 64.7 km**

Beginner, Intermediate

Location

The trail runs from Mankato to Faribault, with parking lots near Mankato, Eagle Lake, Madison Lake, Elysian, Waterville, Morristown, Warsaw, and Faribault. The western end of the trail is located northeast of Mankato, northwest of Minnesota Highway 22 on Lime Valley Road for 1 mile to the trailhead.

Sakatah Singing Hills State Trail is a multiple-use recreational trail developed on an abandoned railroad grade. The terrain of the western half involves rolling hills and ravines, and the eastern half is more level, with much open prairie. Primarily developed for hiking, biking, and snowmobiling, the trail has a dual treadway: one for snowmobiling and one for equestrians and skiers. Wayside rests, picnic grounds, and camping sites are encountered at various points along the trail.

Contact

Department of Natural Resources, Division of Parks and Recreation,
500 Lafayette Road, St. Paul, MN 55155-4040
Metro: 296-6157
Non-metro: (800) 766-6000
TDD metro: 296-5484
TDD non-metro: (800) 657-3929

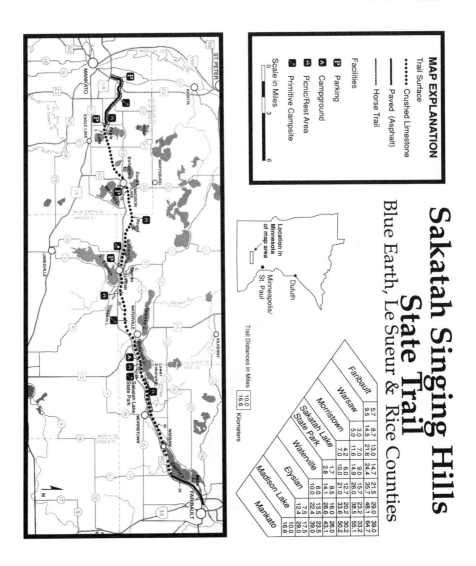

Sakatah Singing Hills State Trail
Blue Earth, Le Sueur & Rice Counties

76 Sand Dunes State Forest Zimmerman, Minnesota

Trackset: 6 km   **Skating: 0 km**   **Ungroomed: 0 km**

Beginner, Intermediate, Advanced

Location
From Minneapolis, northwest on U.S. Highway 10 for 24 miles, north on U.S. Highway 169 for 10 miles to Zimmerman, west on County Road 4 for 4 miles to the parking lot .8 mile past County Road 15, on the south side of the road.

Sand Dunes State Forest was once virgin prairie. When the first white settlers arrived, they began farming the land, and during the drought of the 1930s, the soil of the overused land "took to the air and drifted like snow" over roads and onto front porches. Concerned citizens, in an effort to stop the erosion, planted a variety of trees, including hardwoods and conifers. The conifers survived more readily in the sandy soil, and today they dominate the forest in the area.

The network of ski trails lies on the east side of Ann Lake. Interpretive stations are placed along the trail, and there is a picnic shelter.

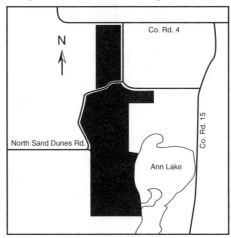

Contact
Department of Natural Resources, Division of Forestry, 12969 Freemont Avenue, Zimmerman, MN 55398
(612) 689-2832
Department of Natural Resources, Division of Parks and Recreation,
500 Lafayette Road, St. Paul, MN 55155-4040
Metro: 296-6157   TDD metro: 296-5484
Non-metro: (800) 766-6000   TDD non-metro: (800) 657-3929

77 Sandrock Cliff Ski Trail
Grantsburg, Wisconsin

Trackset: 0 km   **Skating: 0 km**   **Ungroomed: 8 km**

Beginner, Intermediate

Location
From St. Paul, north on I-35 for 50 miles to exit 165 at Rock Creek, east on Minnesota Highway 70 for 10 miles and just across the St. Croix River, to the parking lot on the north side of the road.

Sandrock Cliff was named for its exposed layer of Cambrian sandstone laid down by advancing and retreating shallow inland seas 600 million years ago. This outcrop was once an island in a much larger St. Croix River. Nearly 3 miles wide in some places, the St. Croix's glacial meltwater carved out a deep and wide valley.

The trail system consists of a series of long, narrow loops along the St. Croix River. Although it was originally designed for hiking, the narrow trail corridor is unlike most ski trails. Even though it is not groomed, skiers will usually find the tracks of previous skiers.

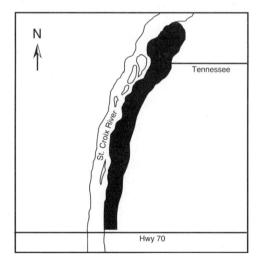

Contact
Village of Grantsburg, 416 South Pine Street, Grantsburg, WI 54840
(715) 463-2405

78 | Sherburne National Wildlife Refuge Zimmerman, Minnesota

Trackset: 0 km   **Skating: 0 km**   **Ungroomed: 14.3 km**

Beginner

Location
From Zimmerman, north on U.S. Highway 169 for 4 miles, west on County Road 9 for 6 miles to parking lot, on the south side of the road, east of the refuge headquarters.

The primary function of the refuge is to protect and perpetuate migratory waterfowl, althought the lush habitat is a sanctuary for plenty of other wildlife as well. In addition, the facility is an excellent resource for environmental education.

There are two trails for skiing, the Blue Hill Trail and the Mahnomen Trail. Neither trail is groomed, but both are well-marked and usually contain the tracks of previous skiers.

Situated in gently rolling terrain, the Blue Hill Trail's wide corridor runs through deciduous and coniferous woods, along marshes, and across fields. It is set up in a system of four loops; one loop has interpretive stations along the trail. There are no facilities at the trailhead.

Its name taken from the Ojibwa word for wild rice, the Mahnomen Trail lies north of Rice Lake. It is a shallow body of water fed by the St. Francis River, and the surrounding marshland supports huge wild rice beds, an important wildlife food source. The smallest trail loop is Mounds Loop, named for the Native American burial mounds found there, estimated at 7,000 years old. This loop has several interpretive stations and an observation tower. The trail winds through rolling hills and a forest of deciduous trees, with some marshlands and fields. Restrooms are available at the trailhead.

Skiing and snowshoeing are allowed throughout the refuge, not just on the trails, but only skiing is allowed on the trails. Snowmobiling is not permitted. No fees or trail license is required of visitors. The refuge is open during daylight hours.

Contact
Refuge Manager, Sherburne National Wildlife Refuge, Route 2, Zimmerman, MN 5539
(612) 389-3323

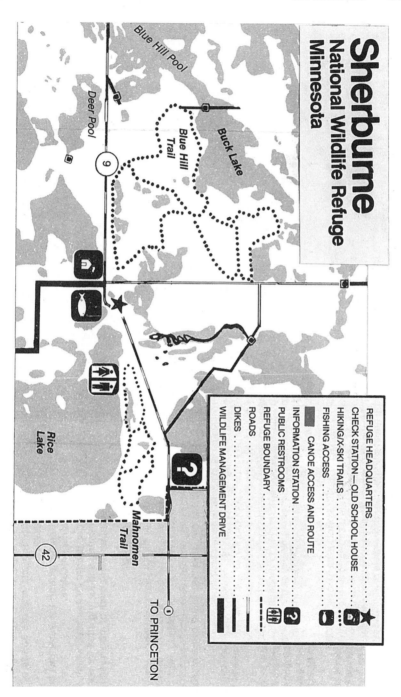

Sherburne
National Wildlife Refuge
Minnesota

Blue Hill Pool

Deer Pool

Blue Hill Trail

Buck Lake

9

Rice Lake

Mahnomen Trail

42

TO PRINCETON

REFUGE HEADQUARTERS
CHECK STATION—OLD SCHOOL HOUSE
HIKING/X-SKI TRAILS
FISHING ACCESS
CANOE ACCESS AND ROUTE
INFORMATION STATION
PUBLIC RESTROOMS
REFUGE BOUNDARY
ROADS
DIKES
WILDLIFE MANAGEMENT DRIVE

79 Snail Lake Regional Park
Shoreview, Minnesota

Trackset: 2.4 km   **Skating: 0 km**   **Ungroomed: 0 km**

Intermediate

Location
From St. Paul on I-694, north on Minnesota Highway 49 (Rice Street) for 2 miles, west on Snail Lake Road for .4 mile, south and west on Snail Lake Boulevard for .8 mile to the trailhead, on the north side of the road.

The trail is a single loop of 2.4 km that runs through mostly forested terrain, with open land at the southeastern end. There are no facilities at the park.

Contact
Ramsey County Parks and Recreation Department, 2015 North Van Dyke Street, Maplewood, MN 55109
(612) 777-1707

Ski Touring Map

LEGEND

WATER

PARK BOUNDARY

WOODED AREAS

SKI TRAIL: INTERMEDIATE

ONE WAY

P   PARKING

SNAIL LAKE REGIONAL PARK

RAMSEY COUNTY PARKS AND RECREATION DEPARTMENT

NORTH

¼ MILE

SNAIL LAKE

SNAIL LAKE BLVD.

VICTORIA ST.

GRAMSIE RD.

MACKUBIN ST.

SNAIL LAKE RD.

STATE HWY. 49 - HODGSON RD.

RICE ST.

1.5 MILES

80 Spring Lake Park Reserve

Nininger, Minnesota

Trackset: 5.8 km   Skating: 2.4 km   Ungroomed: 0 km

Beginner, Intermediate

Location
From the Twin Cities, south on Minnesota Highway 55 for 17 miles, northeast on County Road 42 (Mississippi Trail) for 2 miles, north on Idell Avenue for .5 mile to the trailhead.

Spring Lake Park Reserve is located on high bluffs overlooking Spring Lake, a backwater of the Mississippi River formed by the dam at Hastings. Spectacular vistas are offered on most of the trails in the park. The trails are arranged in a system of connected one-way loops along the Mississippi River and further inland. The skating trail is a two-way loop that runs east from the trailhead and away from the river. The other trails are northeast and south of the trailhead.

The trailhead has a picnic shelter and restrooms, and there are additional shelters along the trail.

Dakota County Parks Rules and Regulations
• Ski in the correct, one-way direction.
• Preserve the wildlife.
• Place trash in refuse containers, and recycle all cans.
• Dogs are not permitted on the ski trails.
• Skating is not permitted on tracked trails.
• Fires are permitted only in designated areas.
• Firearms, intoxicating beverages, and all-terrain vehicles are prohibited.

Contact
Dakota County Park Office, 8500 127th Street East, Hastings, MN 55033
(612) 437-6608

DAKOTA COUNTY PARKS DEPARTMENT
SPRING LAKE PARK RESERVE

Winter Trails

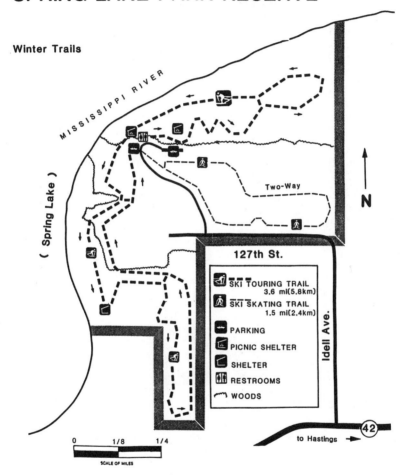

SKI TOURING TRAIL
3.6 mi(5.8km)

SKI SKATING TRAIL
1.5 mi(2.4km)

PARKING

PICNIC SHELTER

SHELTER

RESTROOMS

WOODS

127th St.

Idell Ave.

Two-Way

N

MISSISSIPPI RIVER

(Spring Lake)

to Hastings →

42

0   1/8   1/4

SCALE OF MILES

81 Stanley Eddy Memorial Park Reserve: Northern Unit French Lake, Minnesota

Trackset: 6.4 km   **Skating: 0 km**   **Ungroomed: 0 km**

Intermediate, Advanced

Location

From Minneapolis, northwest on Minnesota Highway 55 for 37 miles to 2 miles past Maple Lake, west on County Road 37 for 8 miles, north on County Road 2 for 3 miles to the park entrance, on the east side of the road.

Scenic rolling hills, lakes, and marshes compose much of the terrain of the reserve. The ski trails range in difficulty from intermediate to advanced, with many steep hills and challenging sections. They run through the hills of the reserve and along the shores of Widmark and Pickerel lakes.

Picnic grounds and restrooms are available at the reserve.

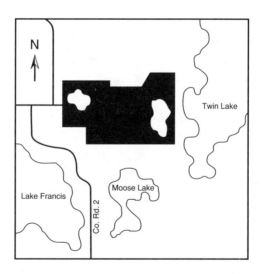

Contact

Wright County Parks Department, 3554 Braddock Avenue Northeast, Buffalo, MN 55313
Local: (612) 682-7693

Metro: 339-6881
Toll Free: (800) 362-3667

82 Stanley Eddy Memorial Park Reserve: Southern Units French Lake, Minnesota

Trackset: 1.9 km   **Skating: 0 km**   **Ungroomed: 1.8 km**

Beginner

Location

From Minneapolis, northwest on Minnesota Highway 55 for 37 miles to 2 miles past Maple Lake, west on County Road 37 for 8 miles, north on County Road 2 for 1 mile to the park entrance, on the east side of the road.

The southern units of the reserve, like the northern unit, are hardwood and pine forest, but the terrain is gentler, with few challenging hills. These trails are well-suited to beginners.

There are picnic grounds and restrooms at the reserve.

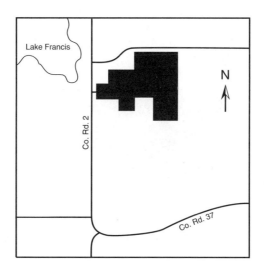

Contact

Wright County Parks Department, 3554 Braddock Avenue Northeast, Buffalo, MN 55313

Metro: 339-6881

Local: (612) 682-7693

Toll Free: (800) 362-3667

83 Sunfish Lake Park
Lake Elmo, Minnesota

Trackset: 13.2 km   Skating: 0 km   Ungroomed: 0 km

Beginner, Intermediate, Advanced

Location
From St. Paul, from I-694, east on Minnesota Highway 5 for 5 miles, north on Stillwater Lane for .5 mile to the parking lot.

Sunfish Lake Park is 285 acres of hilly woods at the northwestern end of Sunfish Lake. Three smaller ponds are also included in the park.

The trail system is a very complicated entanglement of interconnected loops, some one-way and some two-way. Although a few trails are for beginners, almost all the trails run through hilly, wooded terrain and are more suitable for intermediate and advanced skiers. Picnic tables and restrooms are available at the park.

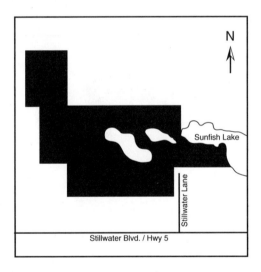

Contact
City of Lake Elmo, 3800 Laverne Avenue North, Lake Elmo, MN 55042
(612) 770-3015

84 Terrace Oaks Park
Burnsville, Minnesota

Trackset: 11 km　　　**Skating: 11 km**　　　**Ungroomed: 0 km**

Beginner, Intermediate, Advanced

Location

From Minneapolis, south on I-35W for 8 miles, east on Minnesota Highway 13 for 1 miles, south on Nicollet Avenue for .5 miles, east on Burnsville Parkway for 2 miles, south on County Road 11 for less than a mile to the trailhead, on the east side of the road.

The landscape of Terrace Oaks Park is composed of hardwood and pine forests, marshlands, many ponds, and gentle to very hilly terrain. From the trailhead the one-way trail runs south. After a short distance, the beginner's loop turns to the left. Continuing to the right will give skiers a choice between the remainder of the main, intermediate-level outside loop and an advanced loop cutoff to the left. All three trails eventually rejoin on the north side of the park. The heated chalet offers maps, rental equipment, and restrooms.

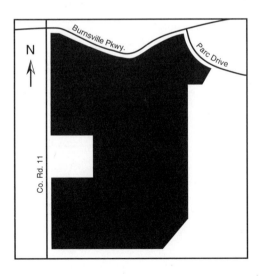

Contact

Burnsville Parks and Recreation, 100 Civic Center Pkwy, Burnsville, MN 55337
(612) 895-4500
Chalet: (612) 890-9182

85 Victoria-Evergreen Park Minnetonka, Minnesota

Trackset: 1.3 km   **Skating: 0 km**   **Ungroomed: 0 km**

Beginner

Location

From I-494 west on Minnesota Highway 7 for .8 mile, north on County Road 145 (Williston Road) for .5 mile, west on McKensie Road for .5 mile, north on Victoria Street for .5 mile to the entrance, on the east side of the road.

The trail is a single one-way loop. There are no facilities for skiers.

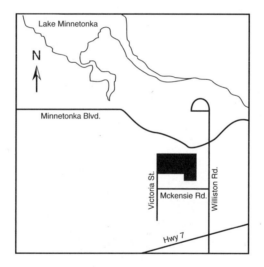

Contact

Minnetonka City Hall, Department of Parks and Recreation, 14600 Minnetonka Boulevard, Minnetonka, MN 55343
(612) 933-2511

86 West Bush Lake Park
Bloomington, Minnesota

Trackset: 0 km   **Skating: 0 km**   **Ungroomed: 1.2 km**

Beginner, Intermediate

Location

From I-494, south on County Road 18 (Town Line Avenue) for 2 miles, northeast on Amsden Road for .5 mile, southeast on West Bush Lake Road for .5 mile to the trailhead, on the east side of the road.

The trail, unmarked and ungroomed but easy to follow, runs through a hardwood forest on the southwest side of Bush Lake, west of Hyland Lake Park Reserve. The terrain is gently rolling, with several downhill runs that are not steep. The trail is not laid out in a loop, so the round-trip is 2.4 km.

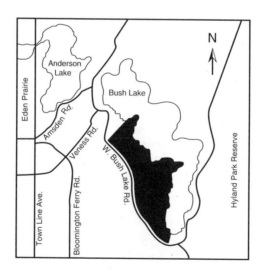

Contact

City of Bloomington, Parks and Recreation Division, 2215 West Old Shakopee Road, Bloomington, MN 55431
(612) 887-9638

87 Wild River State Park
Almelund, Minnesota

Trackset: 56 km   **Skating: 0 km**   **Ungroomed: 0 km**

Beginner, Intermediate, Advanced

Location
From St. Paul, north on I-35 for 37 miles to North Branch, east on Minnesota Highway 95 for 14 miles to Almelund, north and east on County Road 12 for 3 miles to the park entrance.

One of the newer state parks, Wild River's name is derived from the 1968 Congressional designation of the St. Croix River as a National Wild and Scenic River. Along the entire length of the park, the river forms a natural boundary between Minnesota and Wisconsin. For at least 6,000 years, the river valley has been the home of nomadic people, Dakota, Ojibwa, Sauk, and Fox. In recent times, the white settlers developed a major logging operation here. To regulate the flow of timber on the river, in 1889-1890 the St. Croix Dam and Boom Company built Nevers Dam, the largest wooden, pile-driven dam in the world. In 1954-1955 it was dismantled after a series of damaging spring floods, and only the ends of the dam and some of the upstream icebreakers are visible today.

The high quality of this trail system is remarkable. All the trails are clearly marked with degree-of-difficulty and directional signs, with you-are-here maps at all intersections. The trails are regularly groomed for double-tracked, two-way travel. Exceptions to the largely two-way trail system are the southern advanced loop, and a few steeper hills scattered throughout the network.

The amount of trails offered in the park offer a wide variety of skiing experiences. Set in the hills that were once the banks of the St. Croix River, the southwestern section of the park will challenge even the most advanced skiers. This loop of trail should not be attempted by skiers without lots of downhill experience, as most of the hills are very steep and with sharp curves along the way or at the bottom. The trails in the eastern and northern parts of the park run through the floodplain forest of the St. Croix River and inland through prairie. Vegetation throughout the park ranges from dense oak forests to pine tree plantations to maple and birch woods.

Minnesota State Parks General Information
• The parks are open year-round, but the hours vary.
• The use of weapons, traps, or nets is strictly prohibited.

- Pets must be kept on a leash no longer than six feet, and they are not allowed in the buildings or on the groomed ski trails.
- Motorized vehicles are permitted only on the park roads, not on the trails.
- Do not pick or dig up plants, disturb or feed animals, or scavenge dead wood.
- Daily or annual permits, required for all vehicles entering a state park, may be purchased at the park headquarters or the information center in St. Paul.

Contact

Wild River State Park, Route 1, Box 75, Center City, MN 55012
(612) 583-2125
Department of Natural Resources, Division of Parks and Recreation,
500 Lafayette Road, St. Paul, MN 55155-4040
Metro: 296-6157
Non-metro: (800) 766-6000
TDD metro: 296-5484
TDD non-metro: (800) 657-3929

Map following page

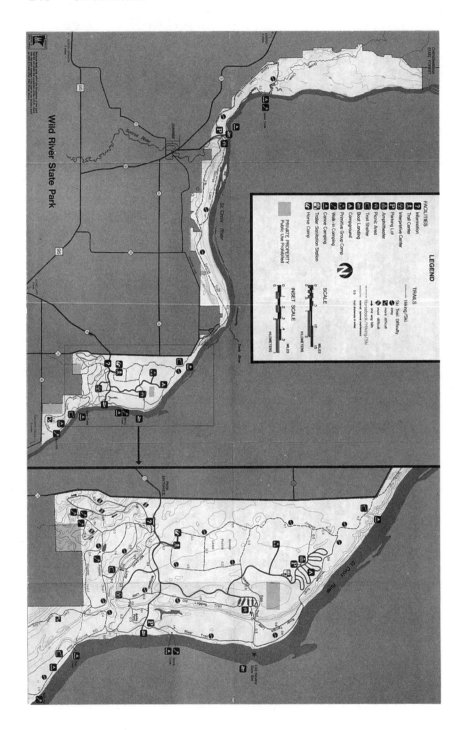

88 William O'Brien State Park
Marine on St. Croix, Minnesota

Trackset: 16 km   **Skating: 13 km**   **Ungroomed: 0 km**

Beginner, Intermediate, Advanced

Location

From Stillwater, north on Minnesota Highway 95 for miles to the park entrance, on the east side of the road.

The scenic bluffs and wooded valley of the St. Croix River are a beautiful setting for skiing and winter camping, the park's main winter activities. The predominant sandstone outcroppings in the park were formed by inland seas millions of years ago. Much more recently, glacial ice covered the land, and in the meltdown and consequent retreat of the glaciers, the released meltwater cut through the soft sandstone, carving the St. Croix River valley.

The park is a wonderful place to ski. The winter scenery is beautiful, and the trails that meander through the forests over the rolling hills will delight skiers of all ages and abilities. All the trails are marked with a number system that is co-ordinated with the park map. Eastward from the parking lot Lake Alice and the river, the easy trail moves through hardwood forest and open land, descending to the floodplain forest of the river valley. The bulk of the trails, groomed for classic and skating, are to the west. The first half of the system, in a fairly easy terrain, is rated beginner and intermediate. Farther west, the skiing becomes more difficult in the upland oak forests, and some demanding stretches on the outer limits of the trail network are challenging even to advanced skiers. There are shelters throughout the trail network.

Ski equipment may be rented at the park.

Minnesota State Parks General Information

- The parks are open year-round, but the hours vary.
- The use of weapons, traps, or nets is strictly prohibited.
- Pets must be kept on a leash no longer than six feet, and they are not allowed in the buildings or on the groomed ski trails.
- Motorized vehicles are permitted only on the park roads, not on the trails.
- Do not pick or dig up plants, disturb or feed animals, or scavenge dead wood.
- Daily or annual permits, required for all vehicles entering a state park, may be purchased at the park headquarters or the information center in St. Paul.

Contact

William O'Brien State Park, 16821 O'Brien Trail North, Marine on St. Croix, MN 55047

(612) 433-0500

Department of Natural Resources, Division of Parks and Recreation, 500 Lafayette Road, St. Paul, MN 55155-4040

Metro: 296-6157

Non-metro: (800) 766-6000

TDD metro: 296-5484

TDD non-metro: (800) 657-3929

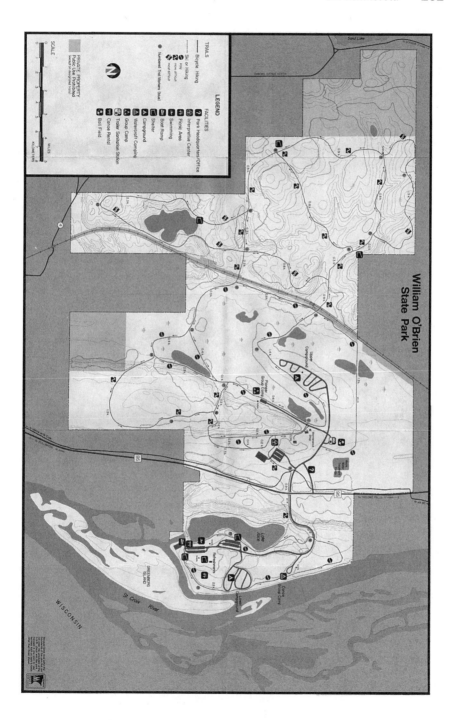

89 Willow River State Park
Hudson, Wisconsin

Trackset: 13 km   **Skating: 13 km**   **Ungroomed: 0 km**

Beginner, Intermediate, Advanced

Location
From east on I-94 across the St. Croix River continuing on I-94 for 4 miles, north on U.S. Highway 12 for 1.5 miles, north on County Road U for 1.5 miles to the park entrance, on the west side of the road.

The trail system is composed of one- and two-way trails and loops through open fields, pine plantations, rolling meadow, oak forest, and past an old graveyard. Some trails run along the fast-moving Willow River to Willow Falls and to Little Falls Lake, created by the Little Falls Dam. Shelter, water, and restrooms are all available at the park.

Daily or annual Wisconsin State Park permits, required for all vehicles entering a state park, may be purchased at the park office.

Contact
Willow River State Park, 1034 Cty Trk A, Hudson, WI 54016
(715) 386-5931

Willow River State Park

Cross Country Ski Trails Map

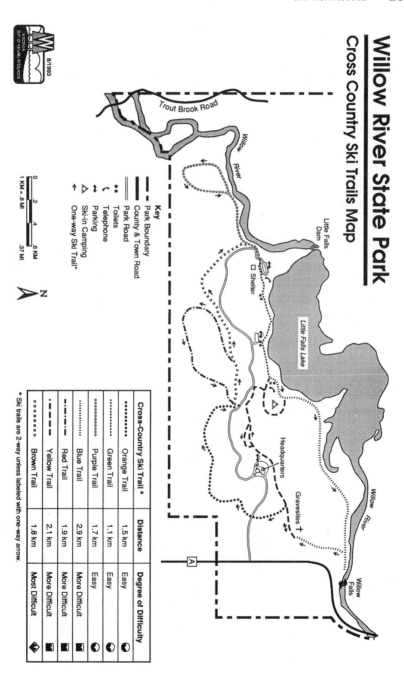

8/1993
WISCONSIN
DEPT. OF NATURAL RESOURCES

Key

— ·· —	Park Boundary
════	County & Town Road
══	Park Road
· : ·	Toilets
☏	Telephone
🄿	Parking
⛺	Ski-in Camping
↑	One-way Ski Trail*

Scale: 0 — .2 — .4 — .6 KM
1 KM = .6 MI — .37 MI

N

Cross-Country Ski Trail *	Distance	Degree of Difficulty	
•••••••• Orange Trail	1.5 km	Easy	●
•••••••• Green Trail	1.1 km	Easy	●
◦◦◦◦◦◦◦◦ Purple Trail	1.7 km	Easy	●
·············· Blue Trail	2.9 km	More Difficult	◑
— ·· — ·· — Red Trail	1.9 km	More Difficult	◑
— — — Yellow Trail	2.1 km	More Difficult	◑
◦◦◦◦◦◦◦◦ Brown Trail	1.8 km	Most Difficult	◆

* Ski trails are 2-way unless labeled with one-way arrow.

Trout Brook Road

Willow River

Little Falls Dam

□ Shelter

Little Falls Lake

Headquarters

Gravesites †

Willow River

Willow Falls

A

90 Wirth Winter Recreation Area Minneapolis, Minnesota

Trackset: 19 km   **Skating: 8 km**   **Ungroomed: 0 km**

Beginner, Intermediate

Location
In Minneapolis and Golden Valley, on Theodore Wirth Parkway between U.S. Highway 12 (Wayzata Boulevard) and Golden Valley Road. The Wirth Chalet is on Theodore Wirth Parkway .8 mile north of Minnesota Highway 55 (Olson Memorial Highway). The MTC Minneapolis Route 20 bus stops at the chalet seven days a week; for scheduling information, call MTC at (612) 827-7733.

Wirth is an especially fine spot for metro skiing. The terrain, very hilly and heavily and heavily wooded, is quite scenic. You scarcely feel city pressures in this enjoyable setting. The trails are in several loops, each designed for a particular type of skier: some cover gentle terrain suitable for the beginner, and others traverse hills more appropriate for intermediates. There are also trails for skaters. All the trails run through the open parkland and woods, adjacent to a downhill ski area and a bird sanctuary. One loop of the trail system is lighted for night skiing until 10:00 p.m. every night.

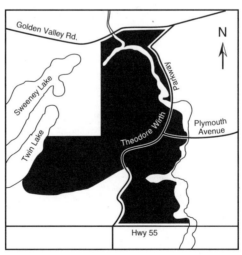

Contact
Minneapolis Parks and Recreation, 1301 Theodore Wirth Parkway, Minneapolis, MN 55422   (612) 522-4584

NOTES

NOTES

NOTES

INDEX OF TRAILS